Confusions in Christian Social Ethics

Ronald H. Preston

Confusions in Christian Social Ethics

Problems for Geneva and Rome

SCM PRESS LTD

0 334 02573 7

First published 1994
by SCM Press Ltd
26–30 Tottenham Road, London N1 4BZ

Typeset by Regent Typesetting, London
and printed in Finland by
Werner Söderström Oy

For My Grandsons
David Preston Kendal
William Peter Cunliffe

and in loving memory
of my wife, Mary

25 November 1915–6 June 1994

Contents

Preface

This book can be seen as an extended case study in Christian social theology and ethics. It raises most of the major problems involved in studying them, not in a systematic presentation but as they have cropped up in the work of the World Council of Churches; and, as a subsidiary theme, in the Roman Catholic Church since Vatican II. The origin of the book is a series of lectures which I was invited to give at the Irish School of Ecumenics in Dublin during the winter of 1992–93 on Ecumenical Social Ethics. It is the only place in the British Isles where ecumenical issues are continuously pursued in depth, and its location in Ireland could hardly be more significant. The lectures were part of the course for students majoring in Ecumenical Studies, who had a good background knowledge. However, there are students majoring in Peace Studies, and it was hoped some would attend, so, for their benefit, I was asked to give a general background to the ecumenical scene. This accounts for the form the lectures took. Subsequently it seemed to me that there might be others who would welcome a broad perspective on a movement of major significance to the churches since at least 1925, within which current preoccupations could be seen in perspective.

The Ecumenical Movement has been a major concern of mine since I was a young man. I had a good start through the Student Christian Movement, for which I can never cease to be grateful. Because of it I was joint Secretary of the Youth section of the vitally important Oxford Conference of 1937. To cover what went before, and has come after that on the 'Life and Work' side of the Ecumenical Movemement in a book of this size has meant a severe process of selection. I am conscious of much that I have had to leave aside, or deal with briefly. And one must remember that there are large areas of the work of the WCC, and of the Vatican, which the theme of this book does not cover.

I have made some severe criticisms of the work of the WCC in the last decade in the area I cover, but there are appreciations of it also. I am conscious that in Britain there is much ill-informed criticism of the WCC. It is not well reported here. Some of the criticism is due to an insularity from which we still suffer, and some comes from those who are anti-ecumenical. It is difficult not to find oneself regarded as an ally of those with whom one has no wish to be associated. It is a risk that must be run. However, let me say here as clearly as I can that I am not an opponent of ecumenism in general or the World Council of Churches in particular. On the contrary I am a strong supporter of both. Indeed my position in this respect is much like it is in the Church of England. I find much to criticize in it, and I long to see the Anglican Communion in a wider ecumenical relationship, but I hope I am a loyal Anglican. It is no service to either the WCC or to the Church of England to be silent when one has thought-out criticisms to make. Time will tell how far they are cogent.

I thank the Irish School of Ecumenics for its invitation and welcome, especially its Director, the Rev. Alan Falconer, who has subsequently become Director of Faith and Order in the WCC. It is difficult to think of anyone with better experience for the job. I also thank the staff and students of the Church of Ireland Theological College, who made my time in Dublin so pleasant, particularly the Rev. Dr John Marsden. The lectures have been slightly expanded and updated since they were given, chiefly because of some important developments in the last twelve months which will carry us on until 1998. But a book cannot hope to deal with yesterday's events; it must take a longer perspective. The appearance of the *Dictionary of the Ecumenical Movement* has made my problem much easier. It is a mine of information with, in general, a high standard of articles. It carries bibliographies. Anyone wishing to look further into issues I raise will find it the best starting point for going on. Also, as one of the editors is a distinguished Roman Catholic ecumenist, it covers a good deal of Roman Catholic material as well, though not nearly so completely as that of the WCC.

I am extremely grateful to two long-standing friends for help in the preparation of this book. Dr Paul Abrecht has read it all. His length of service on the 'Church and Society' side of the WCC from 1949 to 1983 is unrivalled, and his knowledge unequalled. The Rev. Dr Kevin Kelly, of Liverpool and formerly lecturer in Moral Theology at Heythrop College, University of London, has read chapters 3 and 8. They have both tried to save me from blunders and misinterpretations. Responsibility for errors that remain, and for opinions expressed, is mine. My former secretary at Manchester University, Mrs Brenda Cole, has once again coped with the manuscript; she has been involved in the production of all my books since 1975, and her help has been invaluable to me. My wife, Mary, has continued to provide solid background support. We have shared the joys and sorrows of family life for forty-six years; she combines support with a healthy touch of scepticism that academics are inclined to take themselves too seriously.

Once again I have to thank the Rev. Dr John Bowden and the staff of the SCM Press especially Linda Foster, who also prepared the index. As this may be my last opportunity to do so, I wish to pay tribute to the SCM Press. I was a member of its Board of Directors for many years, and for a period I was its Vice Chairperson. It is not easy for a moderate-sized independent, unsubsidized religious publisher to survive, especially when it has a bold and open policy, and does not play safe. I have known all its editors: Hugh Martin, who built it up, Ronald Gregor Smith, David Edwards, David Paton and John Bowden. Gratitude is due to them all, but none has combined so effectively the roles of theological writer, translator and commercial publisher as has John Bowden. I am grateful also to his present assistants, but I name only two from the past: Alexander ('Johnny') Walker who built up the Press with Hugh Martin, and Kathleen Downham, who had served as Assistant to all the editors before she retired.

Ronald Haydn Preston

St Mark's Day,
25 April 1994

Part One

Past and Present

Introduction:
A Preliminary Sketch – The ABC of the WCC

The immediate context of this book is dissatisfaction with the quality of the social theology and ethics coming in recent years from the World Council of Churches. Its more permanent purpose is to investigate 'how to do Christian social ethics' (to put it in a homely way), and to take recent work of the WCC as an important case study. In this area I am particularly concerned with what it is appropriate for churches to do, singly or together, as distinct from what Christians can do as citizens, in their families, their jobs, and their local and wider communities, or what 'unofficial' Christian pressure groups on separate issues can do. It covers what is best done under a distinctively Christian label, and what, in the plural societies which are more and more characteristic of our times, can and should be done in co-operation with adherents of other faiths and philosophies.

The WCC is the chief focus of the Ecumenical Movement. The role of the Roman Catholic Church, which since the Second Vatican Council (1962–5) has been associated in varying degrees with it, will be considered separately. I do not write in any sense as an opponent of it, quite the contrary. All my adult life I have been personally in touch with the Ecumenical Movement, and followed it closely.[1] Indeed, writing from a British background, I am concerned with a certain island insularity which has led to poor reporting of the WCC in the United Kingdom, and a lack of determined engagement with it by church leaders, national and local, in spite of verbal commitment to it. So my case study is not a hostile enquiry, but a challenge to the WCC to do better what its history and resources indicate that it should and can do. It needs to be a beacon to the churches as well as a co-ordinator of inter-church activity.

A case study needs some background. The social theology of the WCC needs to be seen in the context of its history and the range of its activities. Indeed the word 'ecumenical' itself does not trip easily off the British tongue. The word is now much more familiar to British Christians than it was, but it is doubtful whether they mean more by it than a general sense of church congregations from different denominations 'getting together' on various occasions. Nor do they know much of the history of the Ecumenical Movement and the WCC. If the former is dated, as it usually is, from a conference of Missionary Societies in Edinburgh in 1910, it was 1948 before the WCC was officially launched. In 1998 at its next Assembly it will be celebrating its fiftieth anniversary. Much of what has happened since 1910 is not known to churchgoers. Much does not need to be. There is plenty of documentation for those who need it, particularly since the publication of the *Dictionary of the Ecumenical Movement* in 1991.[2] Yet to understand the problems of social theology and ethics in the present, some understanding of the visions and travails of the past is necessary. That is why in chapters 1 and 2 I have tried to distil the main elements which have led us to the present, before looking in more detail in later chapters at the present and suggesting a procedure for future work. In this preliminary sketch I give what the Epistle to the Hebrews calls (in reference to Christian faith) 'the rudiments of the first principles', or 'the ABC', or 'the basic elements' of the Ecumenical Movement, depending on which translation of Hebrews, chapter 5, verse 12 one turns to. Readers who are well aware of this background should skip this sketch and go on to the 'solid fare' later.

1. *What is meant by ecumenical?*

We need to distinguish the modern from the ancient meaning. The Greek word *oikoumene* occurs fifteen times in the New Testament, but its precise sense there does not help us very much.[3] In the ancient world it was used to refer to what concerns the whole inhabited earth (rather like Chinese *T'ien hsia* referring to everything 'below heaven'). From this it narrowed to what concerned the whole Roman Empire; and this sense still survives in the Orthodox Church, where the Patriarch of Constantinople

(Istanbul) is called the Ecumenical Patriarch because Constantinople became the capital of the Roman Empire after the fall of Rome. Then the word came to refer to what has universal church recognition, or nearly so; the early councils of the church and the so-called Nicene Creed, which is at the heart of most eucharistic liturgies.[4]

In modern times ecumenical came into new use as a result of the Protestant missionary movement of the nineteenth century, so much so that it is often called the Protestant century. Problems of church unity became acute when Christian divisions, originating in Europe, were introduced into 'mission lands'. So the word ecumenical came to refer to the relation between two or more churches or confessional traditions in terms of potential unity between them. Going deeper, it came to be realized that the desire for this is for something inherent in the being of the church which is imperfectly realized. 'We who are many, are one body for we all partake of the one bread', as St Paul writes in Romans 12.5 (cf. I Cor. 10.17); or as St John's Gospel presents it, Jesus in his Farewell Discourses prays that all his followers may be one 'so that the world may believe' (17.21). If we take this seriously it sets us apart at once from a popular competitive view of the churches. According to this a united church would be monolithic, too powerful and oppressive, and probably corrupt. (These are certainly dangers to guard against.) How much better to have rival churches, each offering different slants on the gospel to suit different tastes and temperaments. Their mutual rivalry will keep each on its toes. This is a point of view about which we have to decide at the start. If we agree with it we have no use for the Ecumenical Movement.

This, as said by the Central Committee of the WCC in 1951, is concerned with the church as a whole and the wholeness of the church. 'The whole task of the whole church to bring the gospel to the whole world.' In this context 'wholeness' means both the unity *and renewal* of the churches. This is of fundamental importance. Sceptics, faced with the obstacles to unity thrown up by the churches, have questioned the point of 'ecclesiastical joinery'. Let the churches be friendly to one another and each get on with its own life and activities. Other sceptics are simply resistant to change. The church as they know it is a rock of

stability to them in a disturbing and changing world. They see no
need of renewal. However, the point of the Ecumenical Movement
is that unity and renewal go together. Complacency about the
past, and blindness to deficiencies in the present, is no basis for
church unity. That is one reason why a soundly-based social theology and witness is so important. It is essential to a renewal of the
churches.

Since its start in 1948 the WCC has come to find a yet wider
meaning in the term ecumenical: concern for the unity of the
church in relation to the unity of human kind. Here there is much
work yet to be done in re-thinking attitudes of Christians to
adherents of other faiths and philosophies. Modern communications and movements of population have brought Christians into
much closer contact with them. This has been vividly brought
home to a general readership by Hans Küng in his book, *Global
Responsibility*,[5] with his aphorisms: (1) No human life together
without a world ethic for the nations: (2) No peace among the
nations without peace among the religions: (3) No peace among
the religions without dialogue among the religions.

2. *The phenomenon of Christianity and the Ecumenical Movement*

Christianity has vast, varied and rich traditions, and a quarrel-
some history. Quarrels are evident from New Testament times,
notably the turbulent state of the church at Corinth and St Paul's
relations with it. The quarrels arise partly from human intellectual
pride and obstinacy, fermented by economics, political and cultural factors, and partly from the paradoxical heart of Christian
belief itself. Christian faith arose because Jesus' disciples came to
realize that God's reality had been so disclosed in the life and
death of Jesus and the experience they interpreted as resurrection
or exaltation that – devout monotheistic Jews as they all were –
they must worship God through him and in him. So Christians
end prayers with 'through Jesus Christ our Lord'. And they had to
explain to themselves and to enquirers how Jesus, a truly human
person like each one of us, could at the same time be properly and
necessarily worshipped as the unique Son of God. The early

Christians had to think this out in terms of the vocabulary available to them. Paradoxical the faith might be, but it could not be beyond human comprehension. This struggle to understand was difficult, confused and at times bitter, and even violent. Most Christians came to accept what resulted in the so-called Nicene Creed which, of course, has had continually to be interpreted in changing cultural and intellectual situations. Controversies did not end. They were particularly acute, and even bloody, at the time of the Reformation and Counter-Reformation. Churches drifted further apart. Different confessions emphasized different aspects of the faith. Five main confessional traditions have emerged since New Testament times. (1) Orthodoxy, based in the ancient bishoprics of the eastern Mediterranean, and spreading particularly to Russia and later (as have all others), especially to the United States. (2) Roman Catholicism, which is by far the most numerous. (3) Lutheranism; in Britain we are apt to overlook this because it is substantially represented only within the Anglican tradition, but like the others it is global in outreach. (4) Calvinism, or the Reformed tradition; in Britain this is represented by Presbyterianism, especially in the Church of Scotland, Congregationalism and Baptistry. (In England the United Reformed Church is a union of Presbyterians and Congregationalists.) (5) The Anglican; this originated in England and has now spread worldwide, but is the smallest of the main Confessional traditions. Methodism also belongs here, because all its roots are Anglican, but now it has its own traditions and worldwide outnumbers its parent.

However, in addition to these five there are very many other churches. I give some examples. (1) The Peace Churches, such as the Religious Society of Friends (or Quakers) and Mennonites. (2) The Salvation Army, if it can properly be called a church. (3) Unitarians, who have difficulties with the doctrine of the Trinity. (4) Thousands of African indigenous churches, of which the Kimbanguist in Zaire, with five million members, is perhaps the biggest. (5) Pentecostal and Charismatic churches, which now are also influencing the 'mainline' churches.

The WCC, as the institutional expression of the Ecumenical Movement, brings together those of this rich variety of churches who are willing to join it. It pre-supposes that those who do join, recognize at least elements of a true church in the other member churches. The WCC is an emergency enterprise endeavouring to cope with a felt need for unity and renewal, as the weaknesses of the churches amid the complexities and divisions of the twentieth century become evident. In the words of the Message from its first Assembly at Amsterdam in 1948, the churches bound themselves together for this task and said 'we mean to stay together'. The WCC's basis was 'a fellowship of churches which confess the Lord Jesus Christ as God and Saviour'. In 1961 at the New Delhi Assembly this definition was expanded by adding, after Saviour, the words 'according to the scriptures, and therefore seek to fulfil together their common calling to the glory of God, Father, Son and Holy Spirit'.

Three points can be noted about this basis: (1) The term 'fellowship of churches' goes back to a letter from the Ecumenical Patriarchate at Constantinople in 1920 (the office of Patriarch was vacant at the time) to other churches proposing a fellowship of churches, parallel to the nascent League of Nations. The New Testament term *koinonia* which underlies it, is a much richer term than anything possible between nations, a richness which is still being explored. (2) The basis is not to be thought of, and has not been used as a kind of legal or juridical statement; it is more to be thought of as an expression of praise, as when the *Te Deum* is used in worship. (3) The humanity of Jesus is simply assumed and not referred to. The blunt phrase 'Jesus Christ as God' caused some disquiet, and as time has gone on it seems clear that the humanity of Jesus needs to be explicitly expressed.

The WCC as an instrument of the churches does not claim any authority over them. This was established in its early days in the Toronto Statement of the Central Committee in 1950, 'The Church, the Churches and the WCC', where it is said that the authority of its published statements lies only in their truth and wisdom. At times the WCC has found itself almost pushed into living beyond the largely negative parameters of the Toronto Statement, but it has never tried to formulate any statement which goes beyond it. All is provisional, and necessarily so, for the WCC is working to make itself unnecessary.

I now add some background detail.

(*a*) *Who are members?*

Membership consists of about 322 churches, including almost all the Orthodox, Lutheran, Reformed and Anglican, and some Pentecostal churches. The Roman Catholic Church became a full member of the Faith and Order side in 1966, after the Second Vatican Council (which deals with the ecclesiological roots of Christian division), but not of the WCC as a whole. Faith and Order, after years of work, produced at Lima in 1982, an agreed Statement on 'Baptism, Eucharist and Ministry', and has since been working on an effort to find a common expression today of the faith enshrined in the Creeds, under the title 'Towards a Common Explication of the One Apostolic Faith'.

(*b*) *Who are not members?*

Some evangelical churches are in principle opposed to the WCC on Fundamentalist grounds. Organized Fundamentalism dates from the formulation by some evangelicals in the USA in 1895 of four fundamentals, reacting against the growth of historical-critical studies of the Bible in the nineteenth century, and especially against the influence of Darwinian evolutionary theories in science, and their effect on the understanding of the Bible. They also stand exclusively for one particular interpretation of the significance of the death of Christ; this is called the penal substitionary theory of the atonement. Two large churches which remain outside the WCC are in the USA – the Southern Baptists and the Missouri Synod of the Lutheran Church. Moreover there is a minority of members in the 'mainline' churches who are hostile to the membership of their own churches in the WCC. Among evangelical Protestant churches many are members of the Protestant Evangelical Alliance, and there is among them a rival to the WCC, the International Council of Christian Churches, and a more significant World Evangelical Fellowship. But though these are not shadowy bodies their global influence is small and they are scarcely comparable to the WCC in weight and range.[6]

(c) Who has left the WCC?

After the Sharpeville massacre in South Africa the WCC held a Consultation there at Cottesloe in 1961 and, because of its criticisms of the South African government three Dutch Reformed Churches in that country left the WCC. They are now in the process of rejoining. In 1978, after grants from the Programme to Combat Racism (see chapter 2) to certain African Liberation movements, the Salvation Army and the Irish Presbyterian Church also left. The Chinese churches were members at first, but in the years of the Cultural Revolution were forbidden to attend by the Chinese government; they returned at the Canberra Assembly in 1991.[7]

(d) How is the WCC organized?

The basic institution of the WCC is its Assembly, held usually every seven or eight years. Each has had its main theme.

1948 Amsterdam – Man's Disorder and God's Design
1954 Evanston   – Christ the Hope of the World
1961 New Delhi   – Jesus Christ the Light of the World
1968 Uppsala   – Behold, I make all things New
1975 Nairobi   – Jesus Christ Frees and Unites
1983 Vancouver   – Jesus Christ, the Life of the World
1991 Canberra   – Come Holy Spirit, Renew the Whole Creation

The Assembly elects a Central Committee of about one hundred and fifty members, which meets every eighteen months, and there is an Executive Committee of just over twenty, which meets in between. It employs just over 250 full time staff.

(e) Who pays?

Of the undesignated funds, that is to say those not earmarked for special purposes, 97% comes from only thirteen countries, all from North America and Europe (of which the USA and what was western Germany provide 60%). For obvious reasons, very little comes from the Third World. In 1992, 158 churches did not pay their membership dues (though a few paid in kind). There is clearly a danger in such a large proportion of funds coming from just two countries, for money usually means power, negatively as a silent check as well as explicitly. However, there has been little sign of this in the case of the WCC. The churches in the USA and Germany have been wise enough to see that the whole enterprise would be destroyed if they tried to exercise the power which the scale of their financial contributions might warrant.

3. Why take the World Council of Churches seriously?

In 1942, in his Enthronement Sermon, the Archbishop of Canterbury, William Temple, included an often quoted remark that the Ecumenical Movement is 'the great new fact of our era'. He was not exaggerating. There is much that is fine in the two-thousand-year story of the Christian church, but the hatred, divisions and even bloodshed which have been part of it have gravely compromised it. Even today it is in some places an aggravation of conflicts rather than a healing factor. We need to look no further than Northern Ireland and what was Yugoslavia. Leaving aside the vigour of many newly-formed independent churches, the 'mainline' churches cannot disassociate themselves from this history of hostility. Today, though for the most part awake to the need for a new spirit of friendliness between 'separated brethren', they have got so fixed in their inherited structures which they perpetuate, that they regard what they experience as 'normal', and any proposed departure from them as abnormal according to their canon of normality. The WCC is a challenge to these standards of normality, challenging them by what the New Testament clearly intends for the church (though even there it was imperfectly achieved). The teaching of St John's Gospel (especially chapter 17) and the theology of St Paul are powerful in this respect.

In the contemporary situation the WCC is especially important to the churches in the Third World who are nearly always a minority in their countries, and often in an exposed situation. On the other hand the churches of the First World, though less influential than they were, have a weighty institutional ballast which makes it a temptation to make ecumenical concerns an extra to an agenda of long-established items which in practice get priority. The WCC exists to call this in question.

The Ecumenical Movement has certainly produced a vast change in the attitudes of churches to one another (for the most part), and this is indeed a great new fact of our era. The line of least resistance is to thank God for this, stop there, and continue as we are. The WCC has also helped the churches to be much better informed on vital social, economic and political issues in a global perspective, and in that perspective to promote a much better informed and more positive attitude to other major world religions. It has also helped to bring into the open the spectrum of opinions on both doctrine and ethics which in fact exist within all the main confessional traditions (not always officially acknowledged by them). This raises the question how far different traditional divisions correspond to the realities of the situation. So far the institutional barriers to unity have hardly shifted. Where they have, as in the case of the Church of South India, the churches concerned have not had an easy road. Ecclesiastical power politics is much in evidence, more than it is often thought polite to mention, notably the proneness of minorities opposed to reunion to appeal to the civil courts. Many are discouraged, and tempted to regard the Ecumenical Movement as dead, the pursuit of a twentieth-century chimera.

There is a certain worldly wisdom in this. I cannot in conscience subscribe to it. I read the evidence as a call to take the Ecumenical Movement, and with it the WCC, seriously. At the same time I treat it as a call to excellence. It is only by excellence that the WCC can be an effective influence on the churches. Its statements and reports must be seen to have an intrinsic truth and wisdom. That is why the charge by some of its friends that its social thought in the last decade or so lacks competence and credibility is a serious one.[8] It is alleged that the WCC has been too monolithic both in theological approach and in empirical analysis, and has failed to do justice to the diversity of situations faced by Christians, the different opinions they hold, and the variety of methods they employ in their social thinking. Thus it has failed to produce the enrichment brought about by mutual dialogue. It is to these issues that this book from chapter 4 onwards will be addressed. There is no criticism of the basic stance of the WCC in social theology and ethics, in that it is not *other*-worldly (concentrating on the next world), nor *inner-*

worldly (concentrating on the domestic life of the church), but *pro*-worldly (concentrating, within an ultimate perspective which transcends this world, on how human beings can flourish under God in it). It is the parameters within which this pro-worldly stance is expressed which is being criticized.

However, before that can be tackled it is necessary to put the present situation in the setting of what can be learned from the history of the Ecumenical Movement, including the advent of the Roman Catholic Church in it. That is the theme of the next three chapters. Our concern is with the Life and Work side of the WCC. The Faith and Order side, which has been mentioned in this preliminary sketch in order to give an overview of the Ecumenical Movement, is not the focus of this book, but part of its background.

1 An Outline of Ecumenical Social Ethics
1: From its Roots to 1966

Ecumenical Social Ethics takes its place, as the introductory chapter has shown, within the drive for the unity and renewal of the churches which is the aim of the Ecumenical Movement. Its beginnings are usually dated from a world missionary conference in Edinburgh in 1910, in the context of an effort by Protestant Missionary Societies (overwhelmingly British and American) to deal with confusions created in 'mission lands' by the introduction there of divisions between churches originating from Europe. There were already in existence largely lay inter-denominational Christian movements, like the YMCA and the YWCA, but they took little notice of these divisions and were not in that sense church-centred; there was also the World Student Christian Federation, which was church-centred and did take them seriously, and from which most of the early leaders of the Ecumenical Movement were to come.

There was also another body, largely American financed, the World Alliance for the Promotion of International Friendship through the Churches, which was actually founded on the day after war was declared in August 1914, a poignant fact since there was a good deal of pacifist influence in it. Both Protestant and Orthodox Europeans were drawn in, and the experience of such an inter-confessional encounter was quite a new one for them – a foretaste of what was to come. It faded out after the Second World War, but in a sense its legacy to the Ecumenical Movement was the setting up in 1946 of the Commission of the Churches on International Affairs, which continues as part of the WCC, in particular as a Non-Governmental Organization represented at the United Nations.

It is difficult to overstate the isolation of the churches from one another in 1914. They had no sense of responsibility for, or solidarity with, each other, and not much sense of responsibility for 'the world'. There were, of course, exceptions. Roman Catholic social theology had received a new start in the Papal Encyclical *Rerum Novarum* in 1891. The Federal Council of Churches in the USA had been founded in 1907, with a 'social gospel' theological emphasis. In England there was a Christian Social Union and various small Christian Socialist groups. But on the whole there was, in church circles, a fear of social change which still looked back with horror to the French Revolution and the atheist associations that went with it. Very few churches in Asia and Africa were autonomous, and their parent bodies knew little of other confessional traditions, were suspicious of them, and much given to the use of stereotyped labels about them, whilst they competed with one another in a kind of free religious market.[1]

Then came the war of 1914–18. Most European churches combined a robust and uncritical nationalism centred on the Allied cause, or the German one. On the Allied side this was combined with an uncritical idealism that it would be 'a war to end war'. This was echoed in the idealism which set up the League of Nations. It was this which inspired the Ecumenical Patriarchate at Constantinople in 1920 to send an encyclical to all the churches of Christ proposing a *koinonia*, or fellowship, of churches. Despatching this cannot have been easy, for no directory of churches existed. At the same time the Lambeth Conference of Anglican bishops issued a serious call for church unity. The upshot was a meeting in Geneva which laid plans for an ecumenical conference in 1925 at Stockholm on Life and Work, and one at Lausanne in 1927 on Faith and Order. Together these were to be the foundation of the WCC in 1948. Moreover, the fruit of the Edinburgh Conference was the International Missionary Council, formed in 1921. It became part of the WCC in 1961.

By the end of 1920 the Ecumenical Movement was under way. At this time Roman Catholics were not involved; the Vatican had refused the invitation to take part. The Encyclical *Mortalium Annus* of 1928 rejected the Ecumenical Movement; the only road to Christian unity was a return of everyone else to Rome.

1. *Stockholm* 1925

Idealism as to the positive outcome of the 1914–18 war characterized much of the conference. There was a certain optimism that
a united church would prevent war, for it was the Europe of
Christendom which had brought about a world war, whereas
'western' civilization should be a key to world peace, and be the
'soul' of the League of Nations. It was a response to the feeling of
guilt that the churches had done so little to prevent World War I.
A fellowship of churches could be seen as a council or league
parallel to the League of Nations. Archbishop Soderblom of
Uppsala, who was the mainspring of the conference, thought of it
as such a potential council; and also that practical action on the
path of love was a better route towards Christian unity than
the Roman Catholic demand that all should return to the rule of
the Holy See, or the demand of his fellow Lutherans that
all should verbally agree to a confession of faith. So 'doctrine
divides but service unites' was the slogan of Stockholm. One
obstacle, successfully dealt with, was the question of war guilt,
and especially the invasion of Belgium. This was felt to be a key
issue on the Allied side. (This was typified by the story of the
German diplomat who was reported as speculating to Clemenceau
during the armistice negotiations on what future historians would
make of it all, to which Clemenceau replied 'they won't say we
invaded Belgium'.)

There was an Orthodox delegation at Stockholm – a very
important factor in view of the formal separation of eastern and
western Christians since 1054 – as well as Protestant and Anglican
delegates. Only six came from the 'younger churches', which were
the preserve of the International Missionary Council.

At Stockholm there was a cleavage between the more optimistic
Anglo-Saxon attitude to the Kingdom of God being a
reality which it is the task of the church to inspire humanity to
build (a characteristic of 'Social Gospel' thinking), and the more
pessimistic continental, especially Lutheran, emphasis on its transcendence over the 'secular' world. This is often called the issue of
its horizontal as against its vertical reference. Nevertheless, there
was general agreement that social issues should be a concern of
the whole church, not just of enthusiastic pressure groups within

them; and that the often-heard idea is false which holds that the doctrine of the Fall of humanity means that a concern for human flourishing is not part of the church's task. At the beginning of the Ecumenical Movement a blow was struck against a pietistic individualism which was common *in fact* among Orthodox, Anglican and Protestant churchgoers, whatever the more official teaching of their churches. It still is.

Stockholm had no difficulty in listing a whole series of social evils which needed addressing, but it made no economic or social structural analysis. Nowhere in discussing peace and justice are books like Keynes' *Economic Consequences of the Peace* mentioned. Nor did it get beyond its atheism in assessing the significance of the Marxist Russian revolution of 1917.

The role of the laity, a theme which was to be much stressed later, came to prominence at Stockholm. Most churches are in practice dominated by clerics, and male clerics at that, irrespective of their theories of ministry. In this and other ways Stockholm, whatever its limitations, was the beginning of a far reaching ecumenical process. It had to develop rapidly in the traumatic years following the Wall Street crash of 1929. An International Christian Social Institute, with professional staff, was formed in Geneva for the study of Life and Work issues.[2]

2. *Oxford 1937 and after*

The economic depression of the 1930s, with its misery of mass unemployment, was one factor dominating the Oxford conference on 'Church, Community and State'. There were six million unemployed in Germany at the last free election before Hitler seized power in 1933. Thus connected with the depression was the rise of Fascism and Nazism. And in the Soviet Union Stalin was gaining absolute control. There was also the problem of the slight (though important) Christian opposition to Nazism by the Christians in Germany. This was partly due to the anti-Semitism latent in the Christian churches, partly to the fear of Bolshevism and the threat to private property (including church property) which it presented, and partly to the pietistic individualism which, as I have mentioned, was so endemic among churchgoers. All three reasons presented a challenge to the incipient ecumenical movement. It was challenged positively by a small and courageous minority in the German Evangelical (Lutheran) Church, known as the Confessing Church, in their resistance to the totalitarian claims of Nazism. In the German title of the Oxford conference the term for Community was Volk, a key word in Nazism.

Of the four hundred and twenty-five delegates, three hundred were from the USA and the British Commonwealth. Forty were Orthodox, from the USA, Greece and Russians in exile in Paris (for the Moscow Patriarchate discouraged Orthodox attendance); thirty were from the 'younger churches', of which only sixteen were nationals. Among the four hundred and twenty-five were outstanding theologians and church leaders. The conference was well prepared by a process which became classic, headed by Dr J. H. Oldham, an English Anglican layman who had been a leader in the International Missionary Council. Advance papers were circulated internationally for comment, and re-drafting in the light of comments. These papers became the substance of six background books published afterwards, whilst one, *The Church and its Function in Society*, was issued to delegates one month beforehand. A wise commentator said to me, 'If the churches grasp the guts of this book within the next twenty years they will have done well.' In fact a second World War was to speed the process of absorption. Thinking together in this way, with its mutual comment and corrections, by theologians and 'lay' Christians from different religious and 'secular' backgrounds in different continents, about the bearing of Christian traditions in the present context, remains of vital importance in the Ecumenical Movement. Another good feature was that the sectional conference reports were presented for general approval rather than formal adoption. One of them 'The Church and the Economic Order' was so much in demand that it had to be reprinted separately.

In the darkness of the 1930s Oxford expressed penitence for the social failures of the churches, a feature which is charasteristic of WCC documents in social theology and ethics (unlike Roman Catholic ones). It was noteworthy in exploring the relations of love and justice, relating both to the use of power, and showing how justice involves both the restraint of evil and the pursuit of positive goals. The perplexities of Christians and the churches in their attitudes to war were faced, a particular issue in Anglo-Saxon countries where since 1918 theological pacifism was articulated by a significant minority. It was concluded that there is no one Christian position to which all Christians should subscribe. This thinking proved a strength in the 1939–45 war, in which ecumenically-minded Christians never lost touch with one another, and which became in some respects an international civil war.

The general tone of Oxford was what might be called 'Christian realism', in the sense of the pursuit of the relatively best among the possible options (as far as they could be discerned) among particular issues in the search for social justice and peace. It contrasts with the more utopian and idealistic strains which played a large part at Stockholm. Oxford produced the most comprehensive review made by the churches on economic, social and political issues. The churches had become truly contemporary instead of indulging in archaisms, with something powerful to say without tying themselves to any one economic or political system or 'Christian' party, or evading the issues by appealing to an ideal social and political order which bore no relation to the parameters of immediate and necessary decisions. The responsibilities of churches as corporate bodies and lay members as citizens were distinguished and emphasized. In clarifying the relation of the churches to civil society it made clear where a theological issue was directly at stake, as in the treatment of Jews (a foretaste of the apartheid issue). This was distinct from the usual situation where a range of opinions among Christians are to be expected, and the task is to sort out the most plausible views and bring them into dialogue with one another, whilst casting doubts on dubious ones.

Of course this was in a 'western' context. But it was the 'west' which was to provoke a second World War two years later. However, there is much relevant social theology still to be found in the Oxford volumes. The slogan associated with the conference was 'Let the Church be the Church', a phrase from its Message. This was related to a new stress on the church in the Biblical Theology movement, which was gaining ground in Protestant biblical scholarship at the time. There had been a widespread tendency in Liberal Protestant theology to underplay the church, and doubt whether Jesus ever intended to inaugurate one, as distinct from a fellowship of builders of the Kingdom of God. In the sense that Jesus probably had a very foreshortened view of the future he did not found a church as we now experience it, but equally he had no long-term expectation of an ideal social order which humanity was to build. His mission was to gather round him the nucleus of a new community which would recall his people to their true vocation and witness to the radical nature of God's rule, or Kingdom, which would challenge all accepted structures. In 1937 the stress on the church was important as a challenge to the claims of the totalitarian state. Lately some have misunderstood it as standing for a church at the same time introverted and triumphalist. This is a serious misunderstanding. It was a challenge to the churches not to succumb to over-mighty status or to become captive to 'western' culture.[3]

After Oxford, in 1938, seven representatives from Life and Work and seven from Faith and Order, which had held a conference at Edinburgh immediately after Oxford, met together with a representative group of church leaders to plan the formation of a World Council of Churches. Because of the war the WCC could not be inagurated until 1948, in Amsterdam. The legacy of Amsterdam was not seriously challenged until after the Geneva conference of 1966. During the war leading ecumenical figures kept in touch. The clandestine meeting of the two church leaders from Germany, Hans Schonfeld and Dietrich Bonhoeffer, with Bishop George Bell of Chichester at Stockholm in 1942 was a major instance of these contacts. Though their travels the future General Secretary of the WCC, W. A. Visser't Hooft and his colleagues from their Geneva office kept an invaluable webb of contacts in being.[4] In England there was a German refugee Christian community at Wistow in Leicestershire. On the whole the Christian jingoism of the First World War was absent in the Second. After the war the Stuttgart Declaration of German church leaders in October 1945 made forward-looking links and plans possible. After the 1914–18 war it had been 1925 before a similar step was reached.

3. *Amsterdam 1948 and after*

If the context of Oxford was the totalitarian state, that of the first Assembly of the WCC was the post-1945 Cold War. There were

147 churches who became members (now there are 322). Ill-wishers of a 'catholic' persuasion tended to dismiss it as 'pan-Protestant', but it included many Anglicans and Orthodox as the Faith and Order preparatory work had done. The Orthodox from Russia and eastern Europe were not to join until 1961, whilst the Holy Office forbade Roman Catholics to attend; the only ones present were journalists. It was a predominantly 'western' gathering because again it was not until 1961 that the International Missionary Council and the churches associated with it became the third of the basic elements contributing to the WCC. There were a few outstanding Christian leaders present who were not 'westerners', like D. T. Niles and M. M. Thomas. Nevertheless Amsterdam managed to ignore the Indonesian struggle against the Dutch overlords which was taking place at the time.

In the context of the Cold War it avoided lining up with the 'west' against the Communist states, led by Russia. With so much American money behind it this could easily have happened. Moreover it did this without studied ambiguities, but by a reasoned criticism of both *laisser-faire* capitalism and a Soviet style socialism as economic systems both of which promised what they could not deliver. It was in this connection that the term The Responsible Society came into use.[5] This was influential as a basic criterion for the next two decades, and some think it is due for a revival. The term first occurred in the Preparatory Committee and was the brain child of J. H. Oldham. Other terms suggested were 'the human society' 'the free society', and 'the open society'. The Responsible Society was said to be:

One where freedom is the freedom of men who acknowledge responsibility for justice and public order, and in which those who hold public authority or economic power are responsible for its exercise to God and the people whose welfare is affected by it.

The term went out of favour in the WCC because it was thought to be too 'western'.[6] The references to freedom, liberty and justice were disliked by many Christians in the Third World, who liked even less the reference to public order, because they were more concerned with the struggle against oppressive political and economic structures than with the preservation of 'western' democracy. They took it (mistakenly) as being too concerned with the preservation of established institutions. Ironically, some in the USA disliked it for the opposite reason; they thought it too radical, too questioning of liberal political and economic structures.

Clearly consensus, and even dialogue, was to become more difficult as the 'western' character of the WCC began to change. The 'western' churches themselves began to be more conscious of a plural society in their own situation, and with it a more positive attitude to the 'secular' character of that society. Old-style Christendom ways of thinking had to be given up; though the definition and evaluation of the term 'secular' remains controversial and contextual. Indian Christians, for example, regard a secular society, as they understand it, to be essential if they are to flourish.

The second Assembly of the WCC at Evanston, Illinois, in 1954 was notable for a report on 'The Church amid Racial and Ethnic Tensions', the first appearance of this explosive issue (though J. H. Oldham had written a path-breaking book on 'Christianity and the Race Problem' as long ago as 1926). This report caused trouble to the Dutch Reformed Churches of South Africa, but otherwise there was no disagreement on this issue within the WCC, and it dropped from the agenda until action was taken, which went beyond verbal condemnation of racism, by the setting up of a Programme to Combat Racism after the Uppsala Assembly of 1968, to which I shall return in the next chapter.

Following Evanston a study of Rapid Social Change was begun, and continued from 1955 until the New Delhi Assembly of 1961. Evanston had included a report on 'The Responsible Society in World Perspective', and this was designed to fill out the theme.[7] It covered Africa, Asia and Latin America. Rapid Social Change was in reality a euphemism for 'developing'. For the most part political decolonialization had already taken place before the WCC discovered the Third World, and the first contact of many national churches with it dates from this enquiry into the economic and cultural issues facing politically liberated countries.

Rapid social change was bringing about the breakdown of the old order and, except in Latin America, there was no remnant of Christendom to lessen the shock. Nation building, often in countries with artificial colonial boundaries, proved difficult against the force of tribalism, and one-party states seemed a better way than a plurality of parties which tended to have a tribal base. So nationalism, which was under a cloud in Europe for having produced two world wars in this century, was seen as a positive factor in Third World countries, and still tends not to be questioned in WCC documents. Other factors were that churches in Africa and Asia were in a pietistic pre-Stockholm attitude towards 'the world' and some, particularly in Asia, were in a precarious minority situation.

The study questioned any emphasis on *gradual* change. Further, it showed that processes of urbanization and individualization were producing social upheaval (particularly the dislocation of family structures) and the dissolution of cultural roots. One key issue is the education of girls. The study showed that the churches were bewildered by the changes they had helped to create. How were these to be evaluated? Which changes represented a human liberation, to be applauded by Christians, and which a new human oppression? How far should the churches be catalyst and how far inhibitors of change? The churches seemed to be blind revolutionaries, and their theological approaches appeared quite unable to cope.

The New Delhi Assembly of 1961 brought into the WCC, as I have mentioned, the International Missionary Council, and that put the question of rapid social change in the Third World even more firmly on the Agenda. The WCC could not cope with it then, but in 1962 the Central Committee approved plans for a world study conference in Geneva in 1966 which came to be entitled 'Christians and the Technical and Social Revolutions of our Time', and which was explicitly meant to do for the mid-1960s what the Oxford conference had done so well in 1937. A new stage in ecumenical social ethics was to begin.

2 An Outline of Ecumenical Social Ethics
   2: From 1966

Ecumenical social ethics has been described as a precarious and controversial enterprise. There is the inherent difficulty of grasping the heart of traditional Christian doctrines in a modern context; of securing the data and evaluating it in order to comprehend that context (what is going on), both its global similarity and variety; and in letting the two interact. Rapid social change means that past experience and interpretations are not necessarily normative. To reach a common ecumenical mind especially on detailed analyses, may be possible, but is not likely. However, if it can sort out differences and bring the adherents of different views to a fruitful dialogue the Ecumenical Movement will perform an invaluable service to the churches. The Geneva conference of 1966 is a notable example of progress in this precarious and controversial exercise, for it prompted a new and more radical diagnosis which has powerfully affected ecumenical social ethics ever since.

1. Geneva 1966 and after

As I have mentioned, Geneva was a conscious attempt to equal the significance of the Oxford 1937 conference, no longer in the dark days of that pre-war decade with its evident rush to disaster, but in the expansive days of the 1960s. 'Christians in the Technical and Social Revolutions of our Time' dwelt on the more positive side of human capabilities expressed both in technological improvements to the human condition together with the need for, and possibility of, drastic changes in the Third World. Both are a challenge to human efforts. Human beings needed emancipation from bondage to the uncontrolled forces of nature and from

oppression by other human beings. These emphases were similar
to those of the Pastoral Constitution of the Second Vatican
Council, *Gaudium et Spes*, agreed at its final section in December
1965.

Ecumenically the Geneva conference was remarkable in
membership. The Third World was represented in significant
numbers. Africans, Asians and Latin Americans were everywhere
(but few Chinese because of the enforced absence of mainland
China from WCC membership), so that the 'westerners' could not
dominate the proceedings. Orthodox were present in significant
numbers, and Russian was a fifth official language of the conference.[1] Roman Catholic participant observers had mostly been
involved in the drafting of *Gaudium et Spes*. They were active
contributors, and the fact that technically they could not vote was
of little significance in a study conference. There was also a very
strong 'lay' element, and it was the first ecumenical conference
where lay folk outnumbered professional theologians and church
dignitaries. In this respect it was far superior to Oxford. Never
before had the churches been persuaded of the importance of finding and sending their leading lay persons, especially those from
economic and political life, and in numbers equal to those of theologians and church leaders. Nevertheless, there is a difficulty in
securing the continuous attendance of active politicians, or those
involved in the day to day running of industry and commerce,
whether managers or trade unionists. They can be suddenly called
away to deal with an issue back home. This difficulty has bedev-
illed ecumenical conferences as far as the area of social ethics is
concerned, the Canberra Assembly being the latest example.

In the light of its membership the radical tone of the conference
was significant. The contribution of those from Latin America was
a particular shock, especially to those from the USA. It was
the first time many had encountered a theology of revolution,
the forerunner of Liberation Theology, and it was the Latin
Americans, not those from Asia or Africa, who were its
proponents. Revolutionary change was said to be needed, because
the way to anything less drastic was blocked. Moreover liberation for the oppressed is the only way the oppressor can also
be liberated. The need for liberation from sin was not denied, but
it was not in the forefront. 'Conscientization' of the marginalized,

as promoted by Paulo Freire, was heard of for the first time, but it became prominent only after he joined the staff of the WCC in 1969. Christian groups were to be in the forefront of the struggle for this, the 'basic communities', offshoots of the church in Latin America, being the model.

The conference reports were more moderate than the references in the proceedings to revolutionary struggles. But they were poles apart from a common assumption that belief in God means a stress on law and order and the established authorities, and that atheism is to be equated with disorder and revolution (an attitude re-inforced by the Russian Revolution of 1917). Technology was accepted positively but not uncritically. Technological optimists were reminded that human beings need to know themselves as created beings living within limits. They are in the image of God but not themselves gods. The limits within which they must live are not on the borders of life where human imagination and ingenuity runs out, but in the middle of it. The influence of Dietrich Bonhoeffer was strong at this point.[2] Humans are challenged to use their power to control their power.

Can the churches be a catalyst for change within these parameters or will they be essentially inhibitors? How far should they be both? These questions, first posed by the Rapid Social Change study, were not faced at Geneva, and so far have not been faced in ecumenical social ethics.

The great strength of the Geneva Conference was that once again, as in 1937, it helped the churches to be up to date and not archaic, and this time in a global context. Theological and empirical studies illuminated one another, as evidenced by the four volumes of preparatory essays, comparable to the six of Oxford.[3] It established its claim to speak *to* and not *for* the churches. However, many of its members suffered from the disease by which the passing of resolutions produces a sense of significant achievement, and in its closing stage Geneva fell a prey to this, quite unsuitable for a study conference. Internal pressures built up to which it was felt necessary to give way. For the rest the procedures of sub-sections, and sections, the hurried preparation of drafts against pressures of time, and the equally hurried discussion of them in plenary sessions, was a feature common to such ecumenical conferences. To some extent such features are inherent because of the related pressures of cost and time. I shall return to this in chapter 8.[4]

Between 1966 and 1968 it became a question whether the Uppsala Assembly would take on board the radical stresses of Geneva, but it did. Indeed it became the prelude to a series of contextual theologies, for example black, feminist and liberation, which have profoundly affected the work of the WCC. This acceptance was helped by a small but significant consultation at Zagorsk, near Moscow, in the spring of 1968. It was designed to clarify some of the new and startling notes of Geneva. It was jointly sponsored by the Faith and Order and Church and Society sections of the WCC, with the co-operation of the new Pontifical Commission on Justice and Peace. This sponsorship was significant. There have always been those who want to drive a wedge between the Faith and Order and Life and Work concerns of the WCC, or to claim that a wedge in fact exists. Whilst of course it may well exist in the minds of some participants on either side, there is no substance in the charge as far as the whole administration of the WCC is concerned.

The first clarification made at Zagorsk was on the meaning of revolutionary change, the demand for which had been prominent at Geneva. It could, of course, mean violent political upheaval. But it could also mean accelerated scientific and technological change which in some countries may upset a social and political equilibrium without establishing a new one. Moreover, there is the question of how to distinguish a revolutionary change to be approved of (in popular terms 'what God is doing in history') from a counter-revolution, which needs to be opposed. Zagorsk made clear that theology, by itself, cannot remove the ambiguities in political-ethical judgments, whether in a revolutionary situation or not. To interpret 'what is going on' requires interaction between deductive and inductive approaches. Sometimes the term 'dialectical' is used of the relation between the two. This, however, has too much of the Hegelian-Marxist legacy attached to it, whereby change coming about through a continual struggle between a thesis and its antithesis leads to a synthesis containing elements from each but transcending both. This synthesis in turn sets up a new antithesis, and so on. This scheme is too rigid. I think the term 'reciprocal' is a better one for the interaction of basic theological or philosophical convictions with the process of securing and evaluating empirical evidence. These issues will engage us in chapter 8.

It became clear that an understanding of what it means to be human underlies one's basic stance in Christian (or any other) social ethic. Christian faith, continually being thought through afresh, provides the criteria by which empirical evidence on 'what is going on' is acquired and assessed. This Christian understanding of the human overlaps in important respects with the understanding of it in other faiths and philosophies. This is the main point of the traditional Natural Law way of thinking (see chapter 3). Zagorsk clarified the basic issues in a way which has not been bettered since, but without going into the detailed problems of moving from a basic understanding of the human to the evaluation of current issues.[5]

Zagorsk also referred to an attitude which was to become very influential. It is an understanding of God as ahead of humanity, as a call to a struggle for the human, and a promise of human fulfilment; it is in contrast to the thought of God as a brake on human endeavours because of a divine guarantee of security based on what has been inherited from the past. This was the main theme of Jürgen Moltmann's *A Theology of Hope*.[6] It is an important corrective to the heavy endorsement of the *status quo* which has been so dominant in Christian social theology; but it is no direct help in making practical decisions (see chapter 7).

The Zagorsk consultation members did not think that a revolution in any of its senses was likely to occur in advanced industrialized countries, though the possibility could not be excluded, because they would have too much to lose by it, far more than the 'chains' which the Communist Manifesto of 1848 urged the workers to throw off. However, the uprising of youth and students in Europe and North America in the late spring of 1968, shortly after Zagorsk, seemed to ask for world-wide revolutionary political and economic change. Christian youth pressed for this at the Uppsala Assembly, and in subsequent years, but apart from vague references to worldwide 'webs' of oppression at the Nairobi and Vancouver Assemblies, the leaders of the WCC have held back from a full-fledged commitment to it. The collapse of Soviet-style economies has shown, ironically, that it is the chains of this that had to be thrown off, or else allowed internally to collapse. It is a pity, however, that a good deal of rhetoric in recent ecumenical documents has called for totally new economic and international orders and has been so vague as to what is proposed instead, and how to get there. The relative stability of market economies in various forms is, however, all the more reason to take seriously responsibilities for working with the Two-Thirds world and the post-collapsed economies of the Second World.

Following Zagorsk and Uppsala, the Church and Society section of the WCC began in 1969 a study on 'The Future of Man and Society in a World of Science-based Technology', which was to lead to the Just, Participatory and Sustainable Society theme. It reminded its constituency of Robert Oppenheimer's remark that 95% of the scientists in universal history are alive to day; and the vast majority are in the First and Second Worlds.

2. *Uppsala 1968 and after*

The revolutionary implications (in the Zagorsk sense) of rapid social change were taken on board at the Uppsala Assembly. The Papal Encyclical *Populorum Progressio* of 1967 had said that economic development was the new name for peace. Uppsala thought this too sanguine. Rather, it could easily make for disorder. How to act so that it could be creative and not anarchic? Uppsala also said that the transfer of resources from the industrialized to Third World countries was not as important as the needed transformations of their own institutions, transformation which, if it was to be well based, could be done only from within. It also thought that the economies of the industrialized and developing countries were not complementary, but rather that a relation of rivalry and subservience was inherent in the situation. To cope with this some argued that the Third World countries should cultivate economic self-reliance. The obvious inequalities of political and economic power between the 'North' and 'South' led others to adopt the neo-Marxist dependency theory, and to take it as self-evident. It has been powerful within the WCC, but in fact it is as dubious as other Marxist economic theories. The stress on self-reliance needs qualification. I shall return to this in chapter 6.

After a period of quiescence racist issues came to the fore at

Uppsala. After the Sharpeville massacre of 1960 and the Cottesloe consultation in 1961 there had been a further consultation at Mindolo in Zambia in 1964. Here the issue of violence became acute. White people tended to say to Africans 'Your cause is just, but in pursuing it you must use only peaceful means'. Black Africans mostly replied that all publicly organized means of peaceful protest in many countries had been outlawed and only forceful protest remained. They added that since Christians in Europe (and elsewhere) had used and sanctioned the use of force in their own disputes for centuries, why were Africans forbidden to do so? This was hard to answer. Uppsala did not answer it, but identified white racism as the crux, because in most countries it is whites who have the power, and called for a crash programme to combat its institutionalized forms. This led to the Programme to Combat Racism, set up in 1969, financed by a special fund from WCC reserves and an appeal to the churches for voluntary contributions to it. This action-orientated decision by the WCC had far-reaching effects, influencing the tone and content of the WCC ever since. Its implications for official church activities will concern us in the second part of this book.

The Programme to Combat Racism could be the subject of an important case study. Its launch could have been better handled, but that was not the reason for the opposition it aroused in some countries, notably western Germany and the United Kingdom. That opposition arose because, while words condemning racism and apartheid were acceptable, actions to back them up revealed the ambiguities in white reactions which had characterized Mindolo. Grants were given, for example, to the Patriotic Front in Zimbabwe, and to military organizations actively resisting Portuguese overlords in Angola and Mozambique. True, they were given for medical, social and educational purposes and not direct guerrilla operations (and that helped pacifists to accept them), but of course it was said that they released resources for those engaged in guerrilla warfare against white occupying powers to spend on military activities. In fact China and Eastern European countries gave them all the weapons they could use, but no money for medical, educational or humanitarian purposes. However, despite the sharp controversy, the Nairobi Assembly endorsed the Programme to Combat Racism and it has been endorsed ever since.

The racist issue was part of the background of a resolution from the traditional Peace Churches asking the WCC to explore non-violent ways of pursuing social and political change. This eventually led to a consultation in Cardiff in 1971 on 'Violence, Non-violence and the Struggle for Social Justice' which, as we shall see in chapter 8, had important implications for 'how to do Christian social ethics'.[7]

Uppsala also led to changes in the Churches' Commission on International Affairs. The CCIA had been set up jointly by the International Missionary Council and the embryonic WCC after a conference at Cambridge (UK) in 1946. Half of its sixty personnel and most of its staff were Anglo-Saxons. The atmosphere was that of Roosevelt's Four Freedoms (of speech; to worship; from want; and from fear). The two sponsoring bodies appointed the Commission and its staff, the latter representing the WCC and the IMC at the United Nations as non-governmental organizations. (The Vatican, by contrast, is represented diplomatically because Vatican City counts as an independent sovereign state.) Until 1968 the CCIA operated in the tradition of European diplomacy, and largely through Anglo-American eyes. Well aware of the unsophisticated support the churches had given to the League of Nations, and their naiveté about power politics, it was anxious not to make the same mistake about the United Nations, but to support it on the basis of a realistic political theology. It did good work on issues of war and disarmament, and human rights (especially the right to religious liberty), but in the eyes of the Third World it was incurably First World. After 1968 it was reconstructed and moved towards a radical Third World perspective, often non-aligned or anti-'western' on international issues, and with marked pacifist strains. This 'new' CCIA has worked on such issues as militarism, and the social security states (characteristic of Latin America in the 1980s), but it is in a weak condition compared with its past. It is now within the ambit of Unit Three in the WCC structure, concerned with Theology of Life: Justice, Peace and Creation. This is partly due to a strain of unrealism in its thought. In a paper for the Vancouver Assembly it said that the political rights of 'western' political systems had no special advantages over the economic ustice achieved by the soviet style economies; and the sentence 'without justice for all everywhere we shall not have peace anywhere', which is often quoted in WCC documents, comes from the CCIA. Short of the *parousia*, or final triumph of Christ, it is vacuous.[8]

3. *From study to action*

Although, as I have mentioned, the Ecumenical Movement is committed to holding together Faith and Order and Life and Work concerns, there is a latent tension between 'theological' and 'secular' ecumenism, the one preoccupied with traditional issues of Christian disunity, and the other holding that the struggle for human flourishing in a global setting is theologically inherent in the ecumenical task. The job of the WCC is to keep the tension creative. Similarly a tension between study and action has developed. The Geneva Conference and the Uppsala Assembly tried to hold both together. Many 'study' folk supported the Programme to Combat Racism because institutional racism, notably apartheid, is so clearly evil. However, criticisms of J. H. Oldham's 'study' method began to be made. The method continued throughout the 1970s, but it was increasingly challenged. It was charged with elitism. From about 1975 only a small part of the WCC programmes on social issues continued to engage in 'study'. It was replaced by 'action', sometimes called 'action-research'. A good example is the consultation on Political Ethics held in Cyprus in 1981.[9] This rejected previous methods of study and urged participation in the sufferings of 'the people' as they struggle against the illegitimacy of power and for a fundamental transformation of society. Hitherto attitudes within the WCC to *laisser-faire* capitalism and soviet-communism had been equally critical, and the need for freedom and social justice equally stressed; but now a stronger ideological stance developed. Participation with oppressed minorities is the only valid approach to social issues; ecumenical study is seen as a distraction from working for social justice, and from sharing the experience of those actually suffering from social injustice in their anguish.

Several factors fostered this change. The tone of a Humanum study for five years from 1969; the founding in 1970 of the Churches' Commission on Participation in Development (though it has had other stresses); the reconstruction of the CCIA; the further development of Urban and Industrial Mission, founded in 1959 by the International Missionary Council. Also there was the presence on the staff of the WCC from 1969 to 1975 of Paulo Freire, with his stress on 'conscientization'.[10] A reconstruction of the internal structure of the WCC in 1972 furthered this change of emphasis.

The Action-Reflection model, which came to the fore, will be discussed in chapter 8. Here it can be said that it has been too sanguine about the participation of 'the people' on the large technological and economic issues, and too open to pressure groups. Indeed the term 'the people', with its Marxist overtones, represents a simplified class analysis, entirely overlooking the element of truth in Lenin's concept of the *lumpen* proletariat.

4. *Nairobi 1975 and after*

This Assembly was originally to have been held in Djakarta, but second thoughts suggested that this would have seemed provocative in a predominantly Muslim country. However, for the first time, white Christians did prove to be in a minority; 55% of those present came from the Third World. Also 40% were lay, and over 20% were women. For the first time, also, representatives of other faiths were invited as members of the common humanity in which Christians share. Controversies relative to traditional Christian attitudes to other faiths quickly surfaced and have not yet been resolved. Another first was that a Professor in the field of Natural Sciences, Charles Birch of Sydney, addressed the Assembly. And from this point on 'humankind' replaced 'mankind' in the texts which emerged. These exhibited the patchwork which is endemic in producing texts in such gatherings, due to the constraints of covering a variety of large themes, after co-ordinating the work of numbers of small groups, and all in eighteen days.

It was also from Nairobi that on the Faith and Order side 'conciliar' language began to be used. 'A conciliar fellowship of churches' was brought in to supplement the powerful statement at New Delhi, 'all in each place', in which the unity of the church was conceived as:

One fully committed fellowship, holding the one apostolic faith, preaching the one gospel, breaking the one bread, joining in common prayer, and having a corporate life reaching out in witness and service to all and who at the same time are united with the whole Christian fellowship in all places and all ages in such wise that ministries and members are acknowledged by all, and that all can act and speak together as occasion requires for the task to which God has called the church.

Nairobi added:

The one church is to be envisaged as a conciliar fellowship of local churches which are themselves truly united. In this conciliar fellowship each local church possesses, in common with the others, the fullness of catholicity, witnesses to the same apostolic faith, and therefore recognizes the others as belonging to the same church of Christ and guided by the same Spirit.

The force of the phrase 'conciliar fellowship' is to stress that the unity of the church is to be neither monolithic nor federalist. How this is to be achieved remains a continual preoccupation. The phrase has caused difficulties, particularly to the Orthodox, because it has been traditionally applied to churches already one in eucharistic fellowship. It is clear that from this angle the Ecumenical Movement is at a *pre*-conciliar stage. How far it is a fellowship in the New Testament sense of *koinonia*, and more than a Movement (as its Basis claims) can also be disputed, but there is a strong case that the actual experience of living together has demonstrated that it is, and that the churches are challenged to recognize this in their various disciplinary procedures which prevent its proper realization in one eucharist.[11]

Whilst stressing the importance of local congregations participating fully in the Ecumenical Movement, the WCC has continually run into the difficulty of communication 'downwards' to them. Its relation to them, unless they happen to have a participant in an event as one of the representatives of their denomination, is through autonomous national and local Councils of Churches. There is no direct communication from Geneva.

Communication downwards depends upon the zeal and efficiency of denominational structures in passing on, through their regular channels, what their delegates have learned from Assemblies and Consultations. In Anglican terms this would mean to dioceses, deaneries and parishes. This difficulty is one reason why in recent years the WCC has been paying attention to special interest groups which by-pass church structures. This danger of bypassing contact is something to which I shall return in the last two chapters.

These problems affect both the Faith and Order and Life and Work sides alike. Before Nairobi there was an expectation that there would be serious divisions between the 'verticalists' (concerned with the inner realities of faith), and the 'horizontalists' (concerned with effective Christian social witness), but this did not occur, so that the Assembly was not newsworthy to the secular press. There was, indeed, some tension between 'north' and 'south', between 'west' and 'east', but no explosion. The tensions did not prevent anxieties about the political-economic authoritarianism in the USSR being aired for the first time in a substantial debate; despite the delicate position of the Russian Orthodox delegates; a resolution was passed urging the USSR to implement the Helsinki Agreement.

It was at Nairobi that the phrase 'A Just Participatory and Sustainable Society' took over, and provided the framework for work in social ethics until the Vancouver Assembly. 'Just' and 'Sustainable' came from a consultation arranged by the Church and Society sub-unit at Bucharest in 1974 on 'Science and Technology for Human Development'. The growing stress on 'People's power' and 'People's movements' was the source of 'Participatory'. That 'the people' in the Third World are becoming more articulate is all to the good, but how to harness this to the complex issues of running a macro economic policy in a representative political democracy, presents many problems which were not faced before the theme was abandoned at Vancouver. The seeds of the post-Vancouver 'Justice, Peace and the Integrity of Creation' theme were sown here in the insight that there is a connection between our attitude to 'nature' and the way we use it, and our attitude to human beings.

Meanwhile how to control the development of science and

technology for human welfare was seen as a problem for 'capitalism' and 'socialism' alike. Nairobi showed a certain naiveté in its attitude to 'socialism' (as Vancouver and Canberra were to do), and also about a new International and Economic order. There has been a latent assumption that economic growth is a zero sum situation between the First and the Third Worlds, so that if the First World has more the Third will have less. In this connection Transnational Corporations were held to be the chief villains. The WCC conducted a study of Transnational Corporations from 1978 to 1982 which seemed loaded against them by many who had no particular brief for them. Few reading the reports would guess that in the consultations on the theme the East Europeans were the most reluctant to criticize them because their governments were negotiating with some for co-operation in development projects.

Following Nairobi the last of the more weighty study conferences (élitist to those who dislike them) was held at the Massachusetts Institute of Technology in 1979, the theme was 'Faith, Science and the Future'. Half of the 400 present were scientists, the first time a Christian agency had brought so many together. But there were too few social scientists and, as usual, too few managers and administrators. On basic intellectual issues raised by 'western' science for some traditional Christian doctrines there was no clear-cut division between scientists and theologians, but the consultation did not explore these issues in any depth. In discussion of political and social issues there was a notable absence of the scientific utopianism characteristic of much of this century in the 'west'. It was seen that scientific work can easily be corrupted by personal and corporate expediency. It can easily become the tool of the rich world (where 90% of the scientists are), of militarism, and of political repression of human beings. Particular attention was focussed on the development of nuclear energy, the storage of radio-active waste, and the need for con-stant surveillance. It represents a 'Faustian bargain' with respect to the longevity of social institutions. There was a call for a five year moratorium on the development of nuclear energy. But it was accepted that no source of energy is clean, safe and low cost, so that difficult judgments are needed in making practical decisions between the various trade-offs in issues of energy policy.

In this connection the ethics of risk assessment and risk taking is of key importance. Public attitudes to risk taking in different areas are curiously arbitrary (as between road and rail deaths for example). In Section 10 of the MIT Conference there is a discussion of the problems of evaluating risks, the criteria for decision making in unchartered areas, and the extent of our responsibility for future generations. This is unique in WCC material, and it is astonishing that it has not been taken up since. I refer to this again in chapter 9.

Little new was said at MIT about economic issues, but the question of our attitude to 'nature' was gaining ground. There is a reference to 'ecological liberation' and to the oppression of the earth. God links himself in solidarity with us; so must we do in solidarity with nature. Much more of this would be heard in the next decade.[12]

5. *Vancouver 1983, Canberra 1991 and after*

The Vancouver Assembly was the first 'participatory' one, a characteristic which the Canberra one was to repeat and of which more will be said in chapter 9. By general consensus the worship was outstanding in quality, an ecumenical experience for those present and of immense importance. But the content of the reports was thin, and betrayed signs of a utopian naiveté which was increasingly to characterize WCC documents. I have already quoted the sentence 'Without justice for all everywhere we shall never have peace anywhere'. As a statement of eschatological fulfilment, of an ultimate hope and one much more likely to be realized celestially than terrestrially, it expresses a conviction at the heart of the Christian faith that 'in the end' God's good purposes for humanity will not be frustrated. However, as a guide to the careful policy judgments that responsible statesmen and citizens have to make at any given time, it is no help at all. Similarly, the statement that the churches should witness to their unwillingness to participate in any conflict involving weapons of mass destruction or indiscriminate effects ignores the difference between those which can only be used indiscriminately and those which can, but need not, be; and the necessary constraints within which they should be used in cases where the use of force is held to be legitimate. Vancouver was so far from thinking about this as to appear pacifist. Nor does it illuminate the issues of bluff, which at that time were serious and to some extent still are, concerning the legitimacy of possessing as a threat the kind of weapon it would always be illegitimate to use.

After the Assembly the Justice, Peace and Integrity of Creation theme was launched. How this came about remains obscure, since it was scarcely mentioned at Vancouver itself. It was merely cited as one of eight priority areas for the WCC by the Assembly's Programme Guidelines Committee, which did not mention the JPSS programme. As compared with the previous theme Participatory and Sustainable were removed and Peace and the Integrity of Creation came in. Justice remained. It is a necessary but difficult concept to handle in terms of public policy with respect both to distributive and commutative justice (corrective justice is not quite so tricky). Aristotle's 'rendering to each his due' does not settle matters, and its relation to the New Testament understanding of *agape* occasions continual theological debate. Peace has been a constant preoccupation of the Ecumenical Movement. The Integrity of Creation will be considered in chapter 6. A case study is needed on the internal working of the WCC on how this major change, which has been promoted as the focus of the entire WCC activity, came to be launched after Vancouver. The Just, Participatory and Sustainable Society programme was clearly unfinished and, indeed, had barely had time to penetrate the local reaches of the Ecumenical Movement, a process which takes at least five years. There had been controversy at the Central Committee in 1979, in Jamaica, about the JPSS programme, which was never resolved or even pursued.

The biggest event in the Justice, Peace and Integrity of Creation programme was the Convocation at Seoul in Korea in 1990. This was a gathering lasting one week, with 500 or more participants, most of whom were newcomers and inexperienced in ecumenical reflection on social issues, and was inchoate in procedures and content. It ended with four general commitments and ten affirmations. I discuss these in the last section of chapter 5.[13]

The Canberra Assembly of 1991 was even more participatory than Vancouver had been, and its worship was again profound and splendid. But again the content of the reports was thin and inclined to naiveté. The most noteworthy example of this was the recommendation that the United Nations should work towards a universal convention which would ban war as a means of resolving conflicts, oblivious of the fact that the Kellogg-Briand Peace Pact of the League of Nations did precisely that. Its effect on what followed in the 1930s was nil. Such ignoring of power structures in international affairs (and indeed in national and civic ones) seemed to show that the WCC was going back to the relative simplicites of the Stockholm conference of 1925, having learned nothing in between. The theological and ethical weakness exposed in these examples was partly due to two failures of the WCC itself. In 1977 the Central Committee set up an Advisory Committee to study the theological and ethical issues in the WCC programme. In 1978 it reported on the Just, Participatory and Sustainable Society programme and the many differences it revealed, especially on theological issues, but never met again; and a proposed group on 'A Coherent and Vital Theology' was never set up. In 1983 the Vancouver Assembly asked for a Theological Advisory Group representing the different WCC units, but it was never set up. Instead José Miguel Bonino made a personal report as a 'one off' item.

This outline sketch of the development of ecumenical social theology and ethics shows that it is not difficult to state the ongoing problem. It is the problem of how to sustain and foster an unwavering commitment to it, whilst at the same time illuminating the necessary provisional and tentative judgments which have to be made, in the light of a realistic but not utopian Christian hope. Such an outlook provides criteria for acquiring, and assessing, the significance of data on 'what is going on' in the world. It may be easy to state; it is hard to achieve.

3 The Roman Catholic Church, Social Ethics and the Ecumenical Movement

'A new relation between Roman Catholics and Protestants is the most momentous change that has come in the life of organized Christianity in my lifetime.' These words of Professor John Bennett, formerly of Union Theological Seminary, New York, and a leading figure in the development of ecumenical social ethics, would be echoed by many others, of whom I am one. The fact that growth in relations at the centre has slowed down, some of the reasons for which will be examined in this chapter, must not obscure the radical change for the better that has taken place. Locally, previous indifference or often hostility, has largely gone. In over 40% of national Councils of Churches in the world the Roman Catholic Church is a full member. Reserve at the centre in Rome limits, of course, how far a national Roman Catholic Church can move, but the much closer experience of co-operation at national and local levels must surely in the end influence the centre in the same direction.

1. *The Roman Catholic Church and ecumenism prior to Vatican II*

The traditional Roman Catholic attitude is concisely expressed in 1302 in the Papal Bull of Boniface VIII, *Unum Sanctum*. 'It is absolutely necessary for salvation for every human being to be subject to the Roman Pontiff.' So it is not surprising that when the Ecumenical Patriarchate at Constantinople issued its call to the churches in 1920 the reply of Benedict XV was negative. In 1919 he had told a delegation from the Protestant Episcopal Church in the USA (Anglican), with reference to a tentative proposal for a Faith and Order conference, that he prayed that the participants by God's grace would see the necessity of being united with the visible head of the church by whom they would be received with open arms.

In 1928, after the Stockholm Life and Work Conference of 1925 and the Faith and Order one at Lausanne in 1927, Pius XI issued an Encyclical, *Mortalium Annus*, which said that the only way to Christian unity is a return to the true church. 'The Apostolic See can by no means take part in these Assemblies, nor is it in any way lawful for Catholics to give such enterprises their encouragement or support.'[1]

As I have mentioned, there were no Roman Catholics, apart from press reporters, at Amsterdam in 1948. And in 1950 Pius XII's Encyclical, *Humani Generis*, taught that the church as the mystical body of Christ was to be identified with communion with the Holy See.

A change began from the pontificate of John XXIII, in 1958, and Vatican II marked it in a striking way. Observers from other churches were prominently placed, and were invited to make comments behind the scenes on drafts of documents. The Declaration on Religious Freedom saw a major change from the previous position of the Roman Catholic Church that (doctrinal) error has no rights. Then there was the Decree on Ecumenism (*Unitatis Redintegratio*). Beforehand there was some anxiety that the Roman Catholic Church might start its own ecumenical movement. But it did not. It recognized the existence already of the Ecumenical Movement, and made many positive remarks about it. It referred to Roman Catholic principles of Ecumenism (*not* principles of Roman Catholic Ecumenism as had been feared); and urged church members to support it within the parameters it laid down. After Vatican II was ended a joint Working Group was set up with the WCC.

The Pastoral Constitution 'The Church in the Modern World' (*Gaudium et Spes*), which had not been envisaged when the Council began, and was adopted at its close in December 1965, was much in line with trends in the social theology of the WCC in preparation for the Geneva conference in the summer of 1966, and many of the active Roman Catholic participant observers at Geneva had played a considerable part in the drafting of the Pastoral Constitution. It seemed a new era had dawned.

At Uppsala in 1968 Roberto Tucci SJ spoke hopefully of the possibility of the Roman Catholic Church becoming in some way structurally within the WCC, but by 1972 the mood in Rome had changed, and the Vatican said that this would not be so 'in the immediate future'. Since then the situation has been described as 'institutionalized non-membership'. The Roman Catholic Church is a full member of Faith and Order, but on the Life and Work side there has been only a series of joint working groups as a liason between it and the WCC. However, under the immediate impulse of Vatican II and the Geneva conference, an official joint body was set up in 1968 in the area of social ethics, SODEPAX (Society, Development and Peace). It is so significant as a case study that I shall deal with it separately in the last section of this chapter.

2. *The social teaching of the Roman Catholic Church from 1891 to Vatican II*

Throughout the nineteenth century the Roman Catholic Church seemed like an embattled fortress, resisting both the acids of the French Revolution and of industrialism. As the century wore on there were the beginnings of a social movement within the church, as an awareness of the alienation of the industrial worker from it in continental Europe began to be realized. Its founders were aristocrats, like the Marquis de la Tour du Pin. Its attitude was patriarchal and paternalist. It heartily disliked the new bourgeoisie, who had supplanted the landed aristrocracy, undermined the power of the alliance between Throne and Altar, and taken away the Papal States from the Papacy. It looked back to the mediaeval guilds and their corporatism. These they idealized, for in modern terms we would call them producers' cartels. They wanted a stable, not a dynamic, economic and social order, the price of which would have been stagnation. Liberal ideas, furthered by the Enlightenment, such as freedom of speech or religion, had little appeal to them. And the nationalism, often mixed with their patriarchism, could easily become what in this century we would call Fascism.[2]

In this context the new start made by Leo XIII in 1891 in the social Encyclical *Rerum Novarum* caused a shock, particularly because of its backing for trade unions. In other respects it was less shocking. Its stress on private property was very strong, in that arguments from John Locke were brought in to augment the traditional arguments from St Thomas Aquinas and, indeed, it was more unqualified than either. It polemically dismissed both liberalism and socialism as 'materialistic', revealing a trait that persists even in recent social Encyclicals. Its strong point was that the dignity of the human person is such that their well-being must not be left to the vagaries of economic chance, which the 'ideal' model of free market capitalism presupposes, but which, it must be admitted, the document imperfectly understood.

In *Rerum Novarum* there was a stress on Natural Law, a concept not much used in Papal social documents before 1891, and deductive reasoning from it to specify social norms, like private property. Since then there has been a radical revision of Papel thinking on Natural Law, (with the notable exception of sexual ethics). It retains its emphasis that Natural Law is the human mind understanding reality, but with the awareness that human thinking is historically conditioned and that our knowledge is constantly open to re-appraisal and growth. There is also now a much wider range of concerns; world economic development, Third World debt, population growth, the arms trade and militarism, and ecological and environmental issues, to name a few. The tone is less authoritarian on details, which are treated more on the level of prudence in practical decision taking. The parameters of the church's claim to competence are more clearly seen. The teaching causes less of a shock now than it did, partly because there is more of it, and church people are more used to it.

The next social Encyclical in the sequence was *Quadragesimo Anno* in 1931. Two points about it are noteworthy. First, in paragraph 79 it introduced the notion of Subsidiarity which, having lain dormant in public discussion for a long time, has come to the fore in the 1990s in relation to the institutions of the European Community or Union. It makes the point that in the social, economic and political areas decisions should be made at the lowest level practicable in terms of the nature of the issues involved. The implications in the text itself seemed to support

Mussolini's corporate state, as will be discussed later in this chapter. However, in the USA it was used, less plausibly, to support Roosevelt's New Deal.[3] Second, the Encyclical distinguishes 'moderate' socialism from communism, something which even the latest social encyclical *Centesimus Annus* fails to do.

In the United Kingdom the group which most explicitly related to this Papal social teaching was the Catholic Social Guild, 1909–68. Some of its concerns were (1) a fear of socialism, which led it to support the post-1945 Welfare State because it made capitalism benevolent; (2) a disapproval of strikes; (3) advocacy of councils of employers and workers to promote the common good. Subsidiarity was not taken up. The main cause it promoted in the political arena was that of Catholic schools.[4] Plater College, Oxford, which was an offshoot of the Catholic Social Guild, is a source of exploration in Christian social ethics, corresponding in some ways to the secular Ruskin College in that city.

3. *The social teaching of the Roman Catholic Church from Vatican II*

At Vatican II few of those present, including the expert advisers (*periti*), had any close knowledge of social issues, though some were brought into the drafting of *Gaudium et Spes*. In the circumstances the production of *Gaudium et Spes* was remarkable. As in other documents of the Council, old and new emphases lie side by side. (That is why those who, since the Council, are pulling back from its new emphases can quote it in their favour.) Part 1 and Part 2, chapters 1 and 2 move traditionally from doctrine to the world; Part 2, chapters 3 to 5 move from the contemporary context. The Constitution refers to Natural Law only once (paragraph 79), but talks more of humanization, very similar to emphases in the WCC.

Mater et Magistra (actually one year before Vatican II, but conveniently mentioned here), issued sixty years after *Rerum Novarum*, broadens horizons in terms of global injustice. It continues the stress on human dignity, though perhaps with a patronizing tone.

Pacem in Terris (1963) was notable for its new attitude to

Marxism, which became the foundation of the Vatican's new *Ost politik* in relation to eastern Europe and the USSR. The key paragraph 159 is worth quoting in full:

> It must be borne in mind, furthermore, that neither can philosophical teachings regarding the nature, origin and destiny of the universe and of man, be identified with historical movements that have economic, social, cultural or political ends, not even when these movements have originated from those teachings, once they are drawn up and have drawn and still draw inspiration from them. For those teachings, once they are drawn up and defined, remain always the same, whilst the movements working in historical situations in constant evolution cannot but be influenced by these latter and cannot avoid, therefore, being subject to changes even of a profound nature. Besides, who can deny that those movements, in so far as they conform to the dictates of right reason and are interpreters of the lawful aspirations of the human person, contain elements that are positive and deserving of approval?

This last sentence is a carefully artless question, because it affirms what Pope John XXIII's predecessors had denied.

Later, two documents on Liberation Theology were to be issued by the Sacred Congregation for the Defence of Faith but they did not give enough credit to Marxism for its analyses of social coflicts. Flawed as it is, Marxism had some pioneering insights.[5] Two of John Paul II's social Encyclicals, *Laborem Exercens* and *Sollicitudo Rei Socialis* are better in this respect.

Populorum Progressio in 1967 centred in economic colonialism as it replaced the post-1945 collapse of political colonialism. It stresses the urgency of economic development in the Third World.

Eighty years after *Rerum Novarum* the document in celebration of it *Octogesima Adveniens*, took the form of a letter from Paul VI to Cardinal Roy, President of the Pontifical Commission on Justice and Peace and of the Council on the Laity. It is a very significant document. The royal proclamation tone has gone. Use is made of ironic questions. The Pope realizes that the right to be taken seriously has to be earned, not least by a dialogue 'accompanying men as they search' locally on how to deal with the current issues which present themselves.

John Paul II has issued three social Encyclicals. *Laborem Exercens*, 1981, on the culture of work, endorses the Marxist stress on the primacy of labour among the factors of production, and encourages a structure where workers are part owners of the enterprises in which they work. His next two Encyclicals back-tracked somewhat on this.

Sollicitudo Rei Socialis, 1987, came twenty years after *Populorum Progressio*, and *Centesimus Annus* one hundred years after *Rerum Novarum*. The former is noteworthy for its recognition of *structural* sin, thus admitting that in society corporate decision making has to be considered, not just the total of individual decision, and that the structures which characterize it affect the possibilities of human action for good or ill, and can constitute elements in social or class conflicts. It seems obvious, but has not always been admitted. The latter also writes of structural sin, but denies the reality of social or class conflict as contrary to an understanding of the common good. It denies, contrary to *Quadragesimo Anno*, that there is a third way between capitalism and socialism. Ecological issues made their first appearance in this Encyclical.

These two Encyclicals take up a three-dimensional approach to Roman Catholic social teaching (first mentioned in *Octagesima Adveniens*). It says that the church is proposing three things in its social teaching: (1) principles of reflection; (2) criteria of judgment; (3) basic directions for action. I shall have to consider these in chapters 7 and 8. At this point we can ask how they are arrived at. The texts refer to the Bible and church teaching, and also to the work of the human sciences. It is assumed that the latter will agree with the former. That is not necessarily so. How is a conflict between them to be handled?

Apart from these Papal social documents, and that of Vatican II, some others since 1966 should be noted. There is *Humanae Vitae*, 1968. The prolonged controversy over its attitude to contraception has tended to obscure the fact that by its endorsement of the 'rhythm method' the church had modified its teaching that every act of sexual union must have the purpose of procreation. It is now taught that it must be *open* to it. Also it repeats the teaching first found in *Gaudium et Spes* (par. 49) which no longer says that the joy of sexual union is subsidiary to, and an incentive to, procreation; it is now seen to have a relational value in itself. Nevertheless the Encyclical has been a great trouble in ecumenical social ethics, because population questions crop up in many contexts, and the Vatican will not admit or tolerate any other of the varying opinions on the matter held within the Roman Catholic Church. The situation is, therefore, that on this and other issues of sexual ethics the Roman Catholic Church has been most explicit where the WCC has had the least to say (and to which it has not given much attention),[6] whereas the WCC has been most specific on economic and political issues where Rome has been more circumspect.

Another document to note is the report of the Synod of Bishops in 1971. It came in the wake of the stress on collegiality at Vatican II, and had considerable weight. (Since then such Synods have been downgraded.) Its theme was Justice in the World, and in it is found the phrase 'preferential option for the poor (or marginalized)' which has subsequently been so influential. A section from its Introduction has been quoted by so many episcopal hierarchies throughout the world as to give it a certain special status.

Lately, national Episcopal Conferences have in some countries been doing some thinking on social and political ethics on their own. The conference in the USA has carried most weight. In 1983 it produced *War and Peace in the Nuclear Age*, on defence strategy; in 1986 came *Economic Justice for All*, on the economic order. Since then it has been working on the position of women, but has run into considerable difficulties with the Vatican, and the project has been abandoned, at least for the present. Indeed the Vatican has been uneasy about the whole process, not least because its method has been quite different from that of the Vatican. It has invited evidence from any who wish to give it, individually or corporately. It has issued preliminary drafts for public discussion before the final text is produced. The bishops say that they are operating at the level of prudence, where Christians may legitimately differ. Vatican documents are copiously quoted whenever they can be brought in, but the Vatican's way of working is so different and so centralized that it is uneasy on the method, and has exercised a wary eye on the contents. Meanwhile, in 1992 the Australian Bishops' Conference brought out a document, *Common Wealth for the Common Good: a Statement on the*

Distribution of Wealth in Australia, which in its mode of preparation and content seems rather like the work of the US bishops.

4. An appraisal of the social teaching of the Roman Catholic Church

This is not the place to give a critique of the content of Roman
Catholic social teaching since 1891. Something will be said about
this in chapter 7. Here I characterize its nature and formation, with
special reference to how it fits into the Ecumenical Movement.[7]

Basic to its approach to social ethics is the affirmation of the
dignity of the person as central to Christian theology. Here the
Vatican and the WCC are at one. How this is worked out can, of
course, give rise to questions. There is, for instance, the feminist
criticism that Rome has developed its thinking on this without any
significant participation of women, or any recognition of the
social role of fatherhood. Similarly with respect to another central
affirmation, the sanctity of human life. How is this to be interpreted? It is not unqualified in that the taking or giving up of life
is in some instances thought to be justified, or even necessary; and
there can be conflicts between the claims of one life against that of
another. Such issues remain the occasion of ongoing reflection.
The WCC is in the same situation.

Recently there has been more stress on a participatory society,
though it is not applied to the internal life of the church. The
Synod of Bishops has lost some of the weight it gained briefly
in 1971. The role of the Curia needs scrutiny. It is never
mentioned in Roman Catholic ecclesiology, but what originated as
an executive has become a dominant factor in policy making,
self-regulating, self-managing, unaccountable to its exterior
constituency, and legally immune.[8]

Related to this are the paternalistic claims of the church,
though these have seen some diminution in the course of the
hundred years since 1891. However, the church is not considered
part of the problems she addresses, but as riding above the human
melee, and able to deliver admonitions and encouragements
impartially to all.

Vatican II included the Protestant insight that the church is *semper reformanda*,[9] always in need of reform, but it has had little effect on the documents which we have been discussing. The one positive suggestion bearing on the church is in *Sollicitudo Rei Socialis*, which urges local congregations to dispose of surplus ornaments and costly furnishings and devote the proceeds to what is often called 'ambulance work'. (This is not to think of it in any derogatory sense, for it is badly needed, so long as church concern does not stop there, but goes on to examine the causes and prevention of disasters.) One wonders how serious is this Papal suggestion, and how far it has been taken seriously. Do we know any instance of it being acted upon?

How are these Papal documents put together? It is meant to be a confidential process, but some information on drafters leaks out. What are the sources? They all lay stress on the continuity of teaching, though changing circumstances are increasingly referred to. Each contains references to the Bible, to the church Fathers and to previous Popes. Lately there has been an occasional reference to a United Nations document. No other empirical sources are mentioned. No flaws in church teachings are admitted. All this is in marked contrast to WCC documents, in the way they are produced and in their tendency to be critical of the churches and, on occasion, of itself.

The production of *Quadragesimo Anno* is best known because of an article by Oswald Nell-Breuning SJ in the journal *Stimmen der Zeit* in 1971. Pius XI asked the general of the Jesuit Order (the 'Black Pope') to draft a commemorative Encyclical forty years after *Rerum Novarum*. He nominated Nell-Breuning, a leading German Catholic authority on social theology and ethics. Paragraphs 91 to 96 were included at the Pope's request, and it was these which seemed to support Mussolini's corporate state, with which the Vatican had made a Concordat in 1929. (I have already noted that in the USA many thought it endorsed Roosevelt's New Deal.) Nell-Breuning says that on reflection the selection of one man for such a task was a mistake. Three other Jesuits were in fact added by their General to make clearer a rather abstract text, but that does not affect Nell-Breuning's point. He also thought that a number of nuances were lost in the translation from German into Latin. Bringing in a dead language adds a hazard.

Some information is known of the drafters of other Papal

documents, but little in detail. One year before *Centesimus Annus* was issued, a conference of economists was called at the Vatican, and it clearly had some effect on the text, which shows for the first time an understanding of the classical theory of the free market and its implications. This step towards a more open way of preparing Papal documents is to be welcomed. It is sad that there is no forum in the Roman Catholic church where social teaching can be hammered out and cross-fertilization be possible. There is nothing approaching the procedure adopted by the American bishops.

The genres of these Papal documents have shown some variations. *Octogesima Adveniens* is a letter, and benefits from that. *Laborem Exercens* seems to be a personalist-existentialist essay by John Paul II. The audience addressed since John XXIII has been men (*sic*) of goodwill. This is important, because it means that the text must operate at the level of Natural Law. This is a confusing term, especially to those who have not grown up with it, and the subject of considerable debate by those who have.[10] At times it has been used to deduce detailed conclusions from the fundamental formulation that humans should follow the good and shun the evil. Fundamentally it affirms that making moral distinctions, differentiating good from evil and right from wrong, is characteristic of human beings ('natural' to them). Problems arise when detailed claims are made on this basis as when it is claimed that sexual intercourse must be open to pro-creation. All men and women of goodwill are supposed to be able to see the cogency of the detailed 'law'. But in fact they often do not, as in the case of *Humanae Vitae*, at least not on the basis of the arguments put forward in the text. Then the authority of the church has to be brought in to back a teaching which on the theory of Natural Law should not be needed. This does not always work. It is arguable that the authority of Papal documents in the Roman Catholic Church has not recovered from the contro-versy aroused by *Humanae Vitae*. Leaving aside much of value in the text, its arguments on this point lack plausibility to many theologians and large numbers of laity. Infallibility has not been claimed for it or for any of the Papal social teaching, but great pressure is exercised to give interior assent to it, and to say that public questioning of it is not permitted. The Dogmatic Constitution of Vatican II, *Lumen Gentium* says in paragraph 25, after stressing the duty of the faithful to adhere to the teaching of their bishop:

> This religious submission of will and of mind must be shown in a special way to the authentic teaching authority of the Roman Pontiff, even when he is not speaking ex cathedra. That is, it must be shewn in such a way that his supreme magisterium is acknowledged with reverence, the judgments made by him sincerely adhered to, according to his manifest mind and will. His mind and will may be known chiefly either from the character of the document, from his frequent repetition of the same doctrine, or from his manner of speaking.

This teaching has made life uncomfortable for 'loyal dissenters', but has not silenced them. Even within its parameters there may be some room for manoeuvre as to whether Natural Law teaching is to count as 'doctrine'.

Another problem is how to relate Natural Law teaching, addressed to men and women of goodwill, to biblical texts which do not, of course, carry anything like the weight to an outsider of goodwill that they do to those within the Christian tradition. On how to use biblical texts in this area neither the Vatican nor the WCC have achieved much. Texts tend to be picked out if they happen to suit an argument, or appear to, but there is no explicit method of relating texts first to their contexts and then to ours, or of distinguishing those which are virtually timeless from those that are time-bound.

Since Vatican II there has been a vigorous debate within the Roman Catholic Church on the renewal of Moral Theology for which it called; and this includes social ethics.[11] The conclusions of those who are 'revisionists' amount to a revolutionary change. Older manuals are cast out. There has been a root and branch reorientation, more biblical and corporate. This has provoked a conservative backlash. Three examples may be given:

1. Some leading Liberation Theologians and reforming bishops were excluded from the Conference of Latin American bishops in Puebla in 1979 and San Domingo in 1992, after the radical tone of the second of these Conferences at Medellin in 1968, (the first one being before Vatican II).

2. For the most part conservative bishops have systematically

been appointed to vacant sees, seminaries have been more closely looked at, and conservative movements like *Opus Dei* and *Communione e Liberazioni* patronized in Rome.

3. *Lumen Gentium* brought into prominence the term People of God to refer to the church in the sense of being a pilgrim people, accompanying humanity to the fulfilment of God's good purpose for it; this was found to be liberating and exhilarating, but it is being replaced by a stress on communion with the centre in Rome as the main stress in referring to the church. Clearly this will not help the Ecumenical Movement. However, the struggle between various emphases within the Roman Catholic church will undoubtedly continue.[12]

5. SODEPAX: A case study

As I have mentioned, the Roman Catholic Church and the WCC were close together in social teaching from 1965 to about 1972. Hopes for collaboration were high, and were epitomized by the setting up in 1968 of SODEPAX jointly between the Pontifical commission Justice and Peace, a product of Vatican II, and the newly-formed Commission of the Churches on Participation in Development (CCPD), later part of the Justice and Service Unit of the WCC. Its original remit was for three years.

In these years it was very active. A consultation in Beirut in 1968 on World Development mentioned the need to slow down the accelerating global increase in population. This, as has been noted, is not an easy issue for the Vatican to handle, for the teaching of *Humanae Vitae* makes it nervous of suggestions of population limitation, even though it is not ruled out. A further consultation at Montreal in 1969 on the same theme was more critical of First World development. Later in the year at Cartigny, near Geneva, there was a consultation on 'Towards a Theology of Development' which broadened the concepts and showed how issues of political liberation become involved, and that it is much more than the new name for peace (which was as far as *Populorum Progressio* had got). In 1970 there were two more consultations. 'Money in a Village World' was an ecumenical reaction to the second UN Development Decade, and the other was on 'Peace: the Desperate Imperative'.[13]

After the rapid and enthusiastic start of SODEPAX problems arose. When its remit was renewed after three years the Vatican insisted on substantial changes in staff programme, and style of work. The WCC did not strongly resist these demands. In 1976 a programme was launched to encourage local collaboration on the issues raised by the UN's New International Economic Order. It also held an investigation into the Northern Ireland troubles. But it gradually became truncated, despite great efforts by the new and greatly reduced staff. In 1980 it was abolished. The Vatican did not think of it as a centre of joint action but as a means of promoting official statements. It was criticized because it developed direct contacts with local churches, partly through its journal *Church Alert* from 1973–80. In some countries local SODEPAX groups were set up. The Justice and Peace Commission thought it too independent, and CCPD that it was overlapping with its own work.[14] The official account of its demise is that it was the victim of its own success. The reality is that it was more due to internal power struggles within both sponsoring bodies; but it would probably have survived if the Vatican had not wanted to keep such a firm hold on it.

The Vatican and the WCC are very different organizations. The Vatican is highly centralized and hierarchical; the WCC at Geneva is hard to co-ordinate and verges on the fissiporous. In the structures of the Roman Catholic Church there is a paucity of laity, whilst in the WCC there is by comparison an abundance of competent and articulate lay folk, even though it often feels itself to be clerically top heavy.

The demise of SODEPAX was a blow. Events since then have reflected the cooling of relations between the Vatican and the WCC after the immediate impulse of Vatican II. A Joint Consultative Group on social thought and action was in being from 1980, with representatives from the Justice and Peace Commission, the Laity Council and the Secretariat for Promoting Christian Unity from the Vatican side, and a wider representation than CCPD from the WCC side. A Joint Working Group succeeded that, but was little more than a periodic staff contact. These various joint groups had no executive authority, but whereas on the WCC side representatives could be reasonably confident of being able to carry out what was proposed, on the Vatican side everything had to go to higher levels, and there it stayed.[15] The only common statement made by the Vatican and the WCC was a Declaration for Human Rights Day in 1973. However, at the grass roots, local collaboration between Roman Catholics and those of other confessions in the area covered by SODEPAX has increased from next to nothing before Vatican II to quite considerable proportions.

The WCC very much wanted the Vatican to co-sponsor the Convocation at Seoul in 1990 on Justice, Peace and the Integrity of Creation. After considerable delay the Vatican refused. The WCC had probably gone too far in its plans before it approached the Vatican. It is not the best way to promote co-operative activity for one body to say to the other 'we warmly invite you to join us in a project on which we have already decided to embark'. Also from the Vatican perspective the WCC appears inchoate, so that you do not know what you will be landed with if you co-operate too closely with it. The Vatican sent eighteen participant observers (many fewer than was hoped) to Seoul, but they were active, and in some ways the Vatican paid more attention to it than some of the WCC's own constituency. But it was such a confused affair that it must have confirmed the Vatican's hesitation. It does not bode well for the more solid joint work that is urgently called for. This would not be as *simpliste* as Seoul. And it could carry a lot of weight.

4 Critics from Without and Within

If the WCC is doing its job it is bound to be criticized from within the churches and by the secular media. Some of the criticism is inaccurate, and sometimes deliberately tendentious, like the periodic attacks in the *Reader's Digest*, which have been part of an ideological pro-capitalist and anti-communist campaign characteristic of the Cold War, and still not free from trying to find 'Reds under the bed' with which to scare its readers. I am not concerned with these, but with more solidly based critiques. They concern both the content of the documents coming from the various Assemblies and Consultations of the WCC and its internal structure. I have selected five critiques, and within each case attached them to one figure or group, not because they are the only sources of the criticisms concerned, but because they are conveniently representative of that type. Nor do I suppose that each is totally distinct from the others, nor that all for which the critics stand is exhausted by what they say of the WCC.

1. *Why criticisms of the WCC are inevitable*

Each of the main confessional traditions has its own particularisms and vested interests, whether it is World Methodism, the Lutheran World Federation, the World Alliance of Reformed Churches, the Anglican Consultative Council, the Roman Catholic Church with its Curia, or the Orthodox with their efforts to achieve enough cohesion among the autocephalous churches to make the calling of an ecumenical Council possible. Paradoxically the growth of the Ecumenical Movement has made each more self-conscious, more anxious to safeguard the treasures of the past; and to make sure they are not last in any ecumenical initiative. Moreover, within these traditions local congregations are prone to their own particularisms and parochialisms, often preoccupied with the finances to keep themselves going in their accustomed ways, and not taking easily to wider horizons, even within their own confessions, let alone ecumenical issues. The WCC is trying to break into such situations and, as we have seen, has considerable problems in communication between Geneva and local congregations. It can easily be seen both as remote and potentially interfering.

Also the churches of the former Christendom have tended to be associated with the established civic authorities, and their membership to be largely drawn from the reasonably prosperous, stable and successful citizens. The marginalized are not much found among them, nor are they listened to. It is these churches which were foremost in the foundation of the WCC. By contrast, in the years after the International Missionary Council became incorporated in it in 1961, the WCC has had a good record in giving a hearing and a platform to those who are rarely heard in 'established' church circles.[1] It does this partly by gently twisting the arm of churches to include them among their chosen representatives and, even more, in consultations which speak *to*, and not *for*, the churches by using its contacts deliberately to invite them among its own nominees.

In another respect it has been good in bringing in to consultations experts whom the churches marginalize by ignoring. The large number of natural scientists present at the MIT Conference in 1979 on 'Faith, Science and the Future' is one example. Often they are pleased to help, never having been asked before by any Christian organizations.

A further difficulty is that the WCC must basically deal with member *churches*. When there is dissidence within these churches the WCC has problems. An illustration is the difficulties it has had with the Orthodox churches in eastern Europe, and what was the USSR. The broad strategy of these churches had been to go along with their Communist governments as much as possible in order to preserve the structures of the church, in the belief that it had outlasted many oppressive and hostile governments in the course of its history, and would be there long after its present atheist one had vanished. And so it has proved. But there were dissidents who did not accept this strategy, and regarded it as timeserving or even a betrayal of the gospel. Complaints have now come from such folk, particularly from eastern Europe, about the previous neglect of them by the WCC.[2] There is no easy answer to this. The WCC has one answer, cogent as far as it goes. Not everything done by it, in what amounts to diplomacy, can be done publicly, contrary to what some activists assume, and Karl Barth asserted, when he said that because Jesus Christ is the light of the world there should be no secret diplomacy.[3] How far the WCC did engage in this, and with what success, must depend upon work on its archives.

Sometimes there are tensions within the WCC itself as it relates to bitter disputes that wrack the world and its constituency. I have mentioned that T. C. Chao resigned as one of the Presidents when the WCC backed the United Nations' position in the Korean war; and Sir Francis Ibiam, a Biafran, found himself in difficulties in the Nigerian civil war.

We note that internal tensions also arise in the Roman Catholic Church. Indeed no church can escape them. When Vatican II, opened all the preliminary documents prepared by the Curia were rejected, as pressures which had been building up for some time came into the open. Tensions have continued as the struggle to maintain the impetus of Vatican II is meeting resistance, much of it from the centre. Indeed no church escapes tensions. The Ecumenical Movement cannot expect to survive without criticism. It will partly be because, if it is doing its job, it will call into question what many in the churches have come to regard as normal; and partly because it attempts to bring into dialogue those whose first wish is to avoid it lest, as a result of actually listening to others, it might involve some painful adjustments of attitudes and rethinking of policies.

Criticisms also arise because of the internal structure of the WCC. Due to the size of its operation this is inevitably complex. No sizeable structure is ever likely to operate in such a way as never to give rise to internal criticisms of its system. By 'system' I mean what has been described as 'a dynamic grouping of elements organized for a specific function or functions'. All corporate bodies are systems, because they are all organized centres of energy. In order to act coherently the WCC has to define its procedures and its boundaries so that it can oversee the main-tenance of its structures, and assess their efficiency in terms of the relation between their input and their output, and consider their ability to identify stimuli and take appropriate action. I use mechanical terms deliberately, not because the level at which the WCC operates is anywhere near the relatively simple one for which a machine might be designed, but to emphasize that the human and divine issues with which it is involved have nevertheless a certain brute basis which their 'spiritual' character cannot evade. One aim of its operation is to achieve a system which hinders 'family' rows between its members becoming disruptive.

It has a highly self-conscious staff, in which attempts are made to balance confessional traditions, geographical area, age and sex; and to prevent anyone staying so long as to become divorced from their grass roots. Two dangers arise from this. One is a loss of ecumenical memory. As situations change and current preoccupations come to dominate, the accumulated wisdom from the past can be forgotten. One main task of this book is to call attention to this. The other danger is that in order to achieve these various staff balances (and also among those who are asked to be Moderators of committees and consultations), the best person available is not always chosen. If they were, an imbalance would be created. Yet the WCC has to survive by excellence; otherwise it will be ignored. There is no easy solution to this problem; that churches and the WCC itself recognize it as a continual challenge is the best that can be done.

A further problem is the incipient fissiporousness of the different programmes, which have at times totalled thirty or more. Within the whole operation of the WCC they are prone to develop their own connections, and guard their independence. It requires a strong General Secretariat with a strong structure to keep this from getting out of hand. Those appointed to it need, of course, to understand efficiency not as an abstract concept but in terms of the purpose of the WCC. It also requires a wise and competent Moderator of the Central Committee, who is a key figure in relation to the General Secretary. Granted these desiderata, there are various ways in which the different units and sub-structures of the WCC can be related, but they must guard against the kind of overlapping which amounts to competition, and against not clearly integrating new programmes with such old ones as still continue. Failing this, the structures will not work;

there will be dissensions and incoherences from within which will lead to criticisms from without. Every church is subject to similar constraints. It is unreasonable to expect the WCC to be exempt from them, or to be totally successful in dealing with them. Criticisms will recur. Some will be due to genuine concerns and some to ill-will. Let the WCC be alert to what is cogent in the criticisms, from wherever it comes, and not be resentful at the mere fact of it.

2. Five critiques

(a) Uneasy 'western' liberals: David Martin

'Liberal' is, of course, a weasel word. It can be flung about in praise or blame indiscriminately; in recent years more in blame. Its force too often comes from what it is defined against, in particular 'radical' or 'conservative'. Many might think of David Martin, formerly one of the Professors of Sociology at the London School of Economics, as more in the conservative than the liberal camp. But he uses the term liberal himself, and makes quite clear what he means in the passage I am about to quote. It represents an outlook characteristic of many who still attend church in the 'west', where churches have deep roots, and have had a good deal of social esteem and political power, and the unease which they feel when they find it both diminishing and challenged by ecumenical trends as represented by the WCC.

Martin has been referring to 'moderate liberals', whom he represents as being squeezed between the radicals in the command postions of metropolitan communications, and theological conservatives manning the local churches in the provinces. He continues:

> The situation of the World Council of Churches is just another aspect of this and makes still worse the relationship between the 'centre' and the provincial periphery, as well as squeezing out the moderate, old-fashioned liberals yet further. Naturally, the WCC bureaucrats are highly unrepresentative, both in their style and their politics; and their ecumenist assumptions are thoroughly out of tune with the deep rooted attachment to particular forms and localities found amongst most ordinary Christians. The interests of such bureaucrats lie in canvassing

support in the third world, in problems of racism and the like, and their whole theology and vocabulary has decreasing contact with the home constituency. At one and the same time they bureaucratize and standardize and manage to wield an existentialist-cum-Marxist vocabulary of liberation, dialogue, significant encounter and the like. Feeling their own loss of roots they lean ever more heavily towards third world politics, condoning whatever is illiberal in the third world (or indeed in communist countries since they want the prestige deriving from the participation of the Orthodox), while campaigning vigorously against every blot on the social record of their own countries.

(Nairobi 1976, was significant for a break in the silence over communist persecution.) One further characteristic of this higher itinerant ecclesiastical bureaucracy is its espousal of a bureaucratic version of existential language, which issues at the local level in the emasculation of traditional Christian speech, notably the Bible and the liturgy. The mythological elements in Christianity are actually accentuated, *because* they are treated as myths, and then incongruously joined to a flat, official prose style which is regarded as congruent with modernity. The faithful are thus doubly deprived: forced to put up with myth emphasized for its double meaning and made to accept forms of language without rhythm, power or the capacity to evoke. There is one additional difficulty. Both the bureaucratic modernizations of language and the restructurings of organizational forms emanate from *different* bureaucratic sources, thus creating accelerated confusions as to channels and to forms of communication. Nobody knows what to do and everything has to become extremely explicit. Both in clergy and congregations the innovations breed an initial interest, quickly followed by exhaustion.[4]

In many ways this is an astonishing outburst. What is meant by 'naturally' when it is alleged that the staff of the WCC is highly unrepresentative? Of course it *may* be so. But why 'naturally'? There is some hidden assumption here for which no evidence is given. Martin also seems to be inconsistent. Having put himself in the middle between the radicals in the centre and the conservatives at the grassroots, here and in the rest of the passage he makes the outlook of the conservative locals the criterion against which the WCC is assessed and found wanting. It is precisely this outlook which the Ecumenical Movement challenges.

Notice the stress on the words 'bureaucrat' and 'bureaucracy'. As political scientists and sociologists make clear, no organization of more than a moderate size can operate without a bureaucracy. The important point is that it should be efficient and uncorrupt. That is why the model of the British Civil Service has been one of Britain's best contributions to the modern world. True, the word 'bureaucracy' is popularly used in a bad sense (as in 'academic'), but this is thoughtless, and it is pandering to prejudice for a sociologist to use it in this way. It is simply bad sociology.

The interest of these bureaucrats is said to lie in canvassing Third World support, and so they are increasingly out of touch with their own constituency. Again this assumes that a 'western' outlook is the norm and should set the agenda. (Oddly, it seems to assume that all the bureaucrats are from the 'west'.) These bureaucrats practice selective condemnation, condemning the evils in their own countries and ignoring those of the Second and Third Worlds. Scripturally, one might consider it proper to be aware first of the beam in one's own eye, especially as the use of the superior political and economic power of the First World has complicated the problems of the Third World. However, leaving this point aside, there is some truth in the accusation. I shall return to it shortly.

Martin goes on to link his criticism with the lament of those who love (rightly) the beauty of Cranmer's English in the *Book of Common Prayer* of the Church of England (1549, 1552 and 1662), which has had the third most considerable influence on English language and literature, after the Authorized Version of the Bible and Shakespeare, because of its growing supersession by modern liturgies. These lack the rhythms and associations of Cranmer's work, but are more intelligible and also, in places, strike a more joyful note. There are real issues here. How far should public worship be in an archaic language? (Latin is beautifully sonorous.) How far should a classic liturgy be kept in active use, since if it is not used a liturgy really is dead? How plain, not to say banal, in language can we dare to be in public worship? How far is a middle way possible in liturgy? In view of increasing difficulties over language is there a greater role for silence in worship? Such questions as these are important, and must find their place within the wide perspectives of the Ecumenical Movement, but there is no reason for Martin to ally domestic changes in the Church of England, which he dislikes, to a general disgruntlement with that movement. The whole passage is feeble, but it is significant in revealing a defensive reaction against change, and therefore against the challenge of the Ecumenical Movement to inherited assumptions and structures.

Nevertheless, as I have just mentioned, Martin does raise an important and pervasive problem. As the voices of the Third World are increasingly heard in the Ecumenical Movement it has proved a shock to the confidence of the First World with its legacy of the colonial and missionary expansion of the last century. It has produced a sense of guilt, to the extent that 'liberals' (not in Martin's sense) find it difficult to witness to what they conscientiously think to be of value in their 'western' roots, and tend to be apologetic when they should not be, and fearful of the charge of paternalism if they criticize Third World institutions or analyses. It means that it is too easy for Third World representatives to ascribe all their problems to the misuse by the 'west' of its power; whatever it does the 'west' is blamed. There is certainly much for which the 'west' has to apologize. The muted celebrations of the 'discovery' of Latin America by Christopher Columbus in 1492 were a sign of a better balance. But we have not yet reached the stage ecumenically where these issues can be freely or easily explored together in love; guilt on one side and resentment on the other hinder it.

There is also an element of truth in one other item in Martin's attack, though he personalizes it instead of putting it in the context of appropriate structures. This is the influence of the staff in the WCC. Those who work continuously on the job in any organization can easily have too much influence in councils and committees, as against the members who are together for comparatively short periods at meetings. This is particularly so with a global body. It can affect the framing of agendas and the choice of consultants. Good administration guards against this, aided by wise and determined Moderators. My own limited experience of WCC consultations and committees is that the staff in attendance have gone out of their way not to dominate but rather to service the proceedings. But of course they can have had a good deal of influence on who is there in the first place. This is an inherent organizational problem which needs watching and bringing into the open. There is no way of avoiding it within the WCC, or within the member churches themselves.

(b) The New Right: Ernest Lefever

I am not going to deal in this section with the economic ideas of the New Right. These amount to a defence of the philosophy of the free market, and it will be evident from the development of ecumenical social ethics that it has gone in a very different direction, and one which cannot be acceptable to the New Right. I have criticized the economic philosophy of the New Right on several occasions.[5] Here I discuss an interesting political criticism of the WCC by the Director of Ethics and Public Policy Center in Washington DC.[6]

The New Right falls back on the foolish argument that the church should confine itself to 'religious' or 'spiritual' questions, and not politicize the gospel. It is a false distinction to oppose 'spiritual' to what we often call 'material' in this way. A vital part of spirituality is how we use the material. Those who make this distinction usually approve when churches support the established authorities and institutions, and consider that to be non-political; only criticism of them is called political. Lefever is much more sophisticated. Indeed his view of the role of the church is plausible.

First, Christians and churches should support justice, freedom and the rule of law, without identifying themselves fully with any political cause or order, whether the prevailing one or a challenge to it. Second, the WCC should speak *to* and not *for* the churches. His theological and political criticisms arise because of his hostility to the Programme to Combat Racism. He thinks the WCC should have made use of the traditional criteria of the Just War; and had it done so it would have been a herculean task to make 'revolutionary terror' fit it.

He has a point. The WCC has been very weak on Just War studies, and has been much too ready to assume, without discussion, that the Just War concept is no longer applicable. But Lefever fails to notice the twisted history of the use of it by the churches, and the lack in it of serious thought on the criteria for forceful resistance to tyrannous political authorities (though theoretically it was allowed for) including guerrilla warfare. Dismissing it as 'revolutionary terror' will not do. Questions of a Just Revolution are involved.

Lefever is critical of a resolution, passed at the New Delhi Assembly in 1961 by 179 votes to 177, criticizing the Portuguese in Angola. What was gained by it? Also, he thinks that Mazorewa and Sithole in Rhodesia (Zimbabwe) in 1978 had majority support, and that Ian Smith was working to establish a democratic multi-party government on a universal franchise. He was opposed to the struggle of SWAPO in Namibia. These are all a reading of the evidence which differs sharply from that of the WCC when it set up the Programme to Combat Racism. Lefever's position has not stood the test of time.

The problem it raises is this. Granted that Lefever's basic position is broadly acceptable, how is it to be brought to bear on these urgent current issues? There is no escape from making a diagnosis, which depends on assessing evidence. There are inevitable uncertainties in doing this, and the possibility that those who share the same basic outlook may assess it differently. In this case Lefever's judgments differ from those who launched the PCR. Time has shown that his judgments were mistaken. How are such differences to be handled within the churches? Is the fact of difference to preclude collective action by a church in the light of majority opinion of a representative body (I am not thinking of a referendum of all church members)? What church members may do as citizens is a different matter. Is there a middle level between agreed general affirmations and detailed policies on which at least in some cases agreement may be reached? Are there ways in which those who take different detailed positions can be held together in dialogue within the church and the churches. These questions will concern us in chapter 8. Lefever dismisses those who disagree with him as running with the radicals. More percipience than this is needed, for such a summary judgment means that one is not open to dialogue, or aware of the inevitable uncertainties in one's own reading of the evidence, and even more in assessing the probable effects of possible policies. Such questions arise again in Paul Ramsey's critique, to which I am about to turn.

Lefever recommends that WCC statements should be more like Papal Encyclicals. Its staff and its documents should not be so homogeneous ideologically. And it should be less utopian, and realize what at a given moment can and should be mitigated but cannot be changed. There is wisdom in this. But it leads to a wider consideration. How can vision be contained with realism? All churches are faced with this problem.

(c) A 'two realms' critique: Paul Ramsey

Ramsey, the notable theological ethicist of Princeton University, focussed his criticism on the Geneva Conference of 1966.[7] It bears some resemblance to that of Lefever, but is more thoroughly worked out. I have called it a 'Two Realms' critique because, although Ramsey was a Methodist, it makes a very sharp division between the realm of the church and that of the public authorities in the state, similar to the traditional Lutheran doctrine of the Two Realms, that of God's right hand and his left.[8]

Ramsey was not critical of ecumenical social ethics as such. He regarded the Oxford Conference of 1937 as a 'landmark'. But he disagreed with the attitude of his section at the Geneva Conference, particularly with respect to the Viet Nam war. With regard to church conference resolutions, he maintained that it is not the church's business to recommend policies to the secular authorities, but only to clarify the grounds on which statesmen might formulate particular policies. Church resolutions should restrict themselves to Action (or Decision) Orientated Directives.[9] Otherwise conferences tend to ignore the cost of the policies they recommend, and to assume that moral fervour is a substitute for responsible study of alternatives. What they achieve is a religious consecration of strong feelings. Further, they tend to a kind of moral excommunication of those in the church who disagree.[10] This leads to a capricious 'situationism', in which everything approved of is counted as what God is doing in the world.

Ramsey approved of the work of Vatican II in the field of social ethics. But, apart from the contents of what it said, he ignored the fact that it was practically confined to bishops, met for four substantial autumn sessions, and in a highly centralized structure. Geneva had 400 delegates from forty countries for two weeks. These limitations, of course, reinforce the importance of the preparatory work, the conditions under which the sections and sub-sections meet, and the process of drawing up the final reports. These issues have become more acute since the Vancouver Assembly.

Ramsey makes some important points in his critique. Just as in Old Testament times it was a necessity to distinguish true from false prophecy, and no unambiguous criteria at the time prophecies were uttered could be found, so it is today in discussing 'what God is doing' in the world. In particular, in connection with the use of the term revolution at Geneva, how to distinguish an authentic from a false revolution, or counter-revolution. We cannot forget that Christians in Germany overwhelmingly considered Hitler's seizure of power in 1933 as a moral renewal under God after what they regarded as the sleaziness of the Weimar Republic.

Ramsey's criticism of Geneva has force. It expanded its conclusions beyond the time available, beyond the proper bounds of a study conference, beyond the competence of the plenary sessions (in which expertise got lost), and indeed beyond the actual degree of consensus among those present. But in fact the plenary sessions were the least important part of the conference. The preparatory work, and most of the group work, was good. Plenary sessions at conferences and assemblies have to be handled very carefully. They are prone to be barnstormed by pressure groups; and they are liable to accept on the spot resolutions and amendments, through sheer pressures of time and conference fatigue, which need much more careful deliberation.

However, apart from plenary sessions, there are problems with the production of final texts woven out of the work of sections and sectional groups under great pressures of time. Many delegates are often coming to their first big ecumenical event, and even if the preparatory work has been good, may have had difficulty in absorbing it. They find the experience exhilarating but overwhelming. They can speak out of their own experience but find it hard to relate it to a wider context. The role of moderators and advisers as facilitators becomes crucial, and they need careful selection and briefing. Experience since Geneva has reinforced these points.

The trouble with Ramsey's critique is that he makes much too sharp a separation between the 'magistrates' (his term for the civil authorities) and the rest of us, as if they live in a social vacuum, and do not themselves have presuppositions which need to be challenged. The 'Two Realms' theology has important strengths; but it can be overplayed, and the gulf between them made too great. The effort to find a middle level of Christian reflection between general affirmations of social doctrine and detailed policies is designed to bridge this gap. Ramsey himself thinks it can be bridged in extreme circumstances, such as 'at the gates of Auschwitz'; here there can be no disagreement. Such treatment of the Jews must be totally opposed. One might say it is a *status confessionis*, of which Duckrow makes much, as we shall see in the next section. However, few situations are as clear as this. Yet we must still be ready to identify injustices, and take calculated risks in seeking to right them, in spite of ambiguities and uncertainties. This is true both of churches and individual Christians. The churches have been too complacent, too ready to stop at 'ambulance work', which copes with immediate disasters but does not try to deal with their causes. Churches need to get beyond Ramsey's Action Orientated Directives. Concentration on them led Ramsey to underplay the achievement of Geneva. Looking back on it in 1979 my verdict was 'The upshot is that for the first time in centuries the churches (now globally) have available some organized thought on social issues which is up to date to guide them. If they persist in archaic attitudes it will be wilful persistence.'

(d) Radical Apocalyptism: Ulrich Duckrow

Apocalyptic urgency has its effects on decision making. St Paul's answer to questions put to him on marriage by a delegation from the Church at Corinth is controlled by his belief that 'the time is short' (I Cor. 7.29). Some political, economic and ecological analyses today paint a picture of humanly made catastrophes

about to hit us. They have been influential in ecumenical circles. In
the economic and political realm it is a strain in Liberation
Theology, a powerful influence in recent decades. I mention this
first. After that I refer to an economic challenge presented by
Duckrow, the (West) German Lutheran ecumenical theologian.
The ecological and environmental challenge will be dealt with
when the concept 'the integrity of Creation' is considered in
chapters 6 and 7. It might seem odd to include Duckrow as a critic
of the WCC since he has had so much influence on it as
a consultant for more than a decade, and it publishes his books.
His criticism is that it is not more radical, because of the resistance
from the representatives the 'western' churches send to it; they do
not agree with his analyses

Liberation theology is concerned with *orthopraxis*, a term with
Marxist overtones, but with biblical roots in a passage such as the
allegory of the sheep and the goats in Matthew 25. Its charge is
that without action with and for the poor we turn the gospel into
an ideology of the comfortable. We misread it. But *what* action?
That brings us back to a diagnosis of the factors at work in our
present situation, and what is a fitting response to it. An estimate
of the likely consequences of what is proposed is involved.
Liberation theologians tend to turn to versions of Marxist theories
for their diagnoses, assuming that they are well grounded, without
examining them. Further, the term *orthopraxis* suggests the
Marxist slogan of the unity of theory and practice, whereas in
Christian thought the reality is that we continually do what we
should not do, and leave undone what we should do, so that in
our life there is always a gulf between theory and practice. We
continually need the renewal of forgiveness, and a radical vision
transcending the present state of affairs to prevent us settling
down complacently as forgiven sinners.[11] Christian faith gives us
an eschatological hope that the good work which God has begun
in creation with humanity he will complete, but we do not know
how or when.

The radical critics of the WCC have an eschatological hope
beyond their immediate apocalyptic judgment on the *status quo*.
How is it to be immediately implemented? We get utopian
demands for the banning of war, the adoption of Gandhian
life styles, and an economic order based on co-operatives not

competition. Allied with this has been the demand by Duckrow that the evils of the 'western' economic system be declared a *status confessionis* by the churches.[12] This is a Reformation term, occurring in the Formula of Concord (1577) to differentiate matters vital to the being of the church from matters of indifference (*adiaphora*), such as the vestments of the ministers in public worship. Now a much wider use is proposed. In the 1950s Barth suggested it should be applied to German rearmament.[13] Recent candidates have been militarism and the arms trade, weapons of mass destruction, white racism, capitalism (called demonic by Duckrow), the First World's captivity to consumerism instead of zero economic growth, and transnational corporations as oppressors of the two-thirds world. This is a bizarre mishmash of issues.

The term *status confessionis* was not used in connection with a political issue until Bonhoeffer raised it after the Nazis came to power in 1933. But he did not carry even the Confessing Church with him. The famous Barmen Declaration of 1934 did not refer to the Jewish question, or to any specific issue external to the inner life of the church. It is possible to see it extended to an extreme version of the Two Realms theory, which in a pietistic fashion might declare that political and economic issues are a matter of indifference to Christians. It is possible to see that called a heresy. It is possible to agree that apartheid be declared a *status confessionis*, as the Lutheran World Federation did in 1977 and the World Alliance of Reformed Churches did in 1982. Apartheid was not set up because blacks wanted 'separate development', within a wider state of which they approved, to give them a 'space' of their own. It was imposed on them by brute force by a state in which they had no say. This separation on race and colour grounds was being defended within the Dutch Reformed Churches of South Africa on Christian grounds. It could properly be called a heresy. But it is extremely difficult to see other issues to which it could apply. Even in the case of weapons of mass destruction (which it would be illegitimate to use), it does not cover whether the possession of them as a threat is legitimate. It is much too blunt an instrument to cope with issues which need a closer analysis than the simpliste formulations on which the *status confessionis* concept relies. It will not do to claim that the Justice, Peace and Integrity of Creation process is of the *esse* (or being) of the church,

as *Costly Unity*, a WCC document issued in preparation for the
Faith and Order Conference at Compostela in Spain in 1993,
implies.[14]

(e) *Christian realism: the Vancouver-Berlin-Manchester group*

Dissatisfied with the social theology coming from the WCC since
the Vancouver Assembly, and seeing little sign of improvement, an
informal group of some friends of the WCC, most of them of long
standing and closely associated with it, formed an *ad hoc* group
which met to consider what could be done, at Vancouver in 1990,
Berlin in 1992 and Manchester in 1993. After the Vancouver
meeting an Open Letter was addressed to Emilio Castro, the
General Secretary of the WCC, to which he referred in his Report
to the Canberra Assembly in 1991.[15] After the Berlin meeting,
a pamphlet 'The Future of Ecumenical Social Thought' was
issued for private circulation to any who were concerned, such as
members of the WCC Central Committee. After the Manchester
meeting a letter was sent to the newly elected General Secretary,
Konrad Raiser, on behalf of the group by Dr John Habgood, the
Archbishop of York, who chaired it.[16] I have attached the name
Christian Realist to it because all the members of the group were
committed to the radical challenge of the gospel to social,
economic and political injustices, but also to allowing for the
parameters within which those in public positions in plural
societies must move, especially if they have to satisfy a majority of
the electorate. There are constraints on the use of their power,
trade-offs to reckon with in the policies they pursue, and certain
conserving necessities imposed upon them. The constraints as well
as the challenges are both seen as aspects of God's creative
purpose for human fulfilment.

The criticism of the group is that the WCC has lost ground as a
facilitator in this whole area because its social theology and ethics
has lost the quality of dialogue, analysis and study. I mention each
in turn.

   1. *Dialogue*: Churches and Christians need both to engage in
dialogue with one another and engage in dialogue with 'outsiders'.
It is a process of cross-fertilization and mutual correction. This

does not lessen the force of the need to act against injustice. It does not mean a perpetual sitting on the fence, balancing one consideration against another, and stopping there. How to avoid this is a precise ecumenical concern, but it will alter the framework and procedures of understanding within which action is taken. We need each other, especially when we disagree and irritate one another. We all draw upon the hope that our work will not be in vain 'in the Lord' (I Cor. 15.58), but it will not be the utopianism that, for instance, is nostalgic for the socialism which it still believes was hidden and distorted in the soviet-style economies, nor will it be so naive in its confidence in the power of 'the people' as an undifferentiated entity, nor as suspicious of all uses of power in established structures.

2. *Analysis*: Evidence from many individuals and groups is needed, not all of the same type and tone. An element of this involves expertise, which itself has not to be taken uncritically, but which must not be dismissed as elitist. The tone of the Seoul Report, with its vast assertions 'we affirm', 'we resist', 'we commit', is allied to a woefully inadequate harvest of the preparatory process, even if it has a place in the whole spectrum of Christian social witness.

In analysis special interest groups have a place as givers of evidence, but they are not more important than input from representatives of the churches. However, nothing I have written lessens the need to listen to the poor and marginalized, to give a voice to the voiceless. But that is not the same as endorsing everything they want done. Without an element of expert analysis it is only too easy to advocate policies which would in fact harm them. Apocalyptic warnings of catastrophe are necessary if they are well supported by evidence, and do not derive from a practice of always taking a worst case analysis, as in several recent WCC documents. Moreover, analysis is never concluded. It is an ongoing process. Even as some issues begin to be cleared up, others arise. Nothing is achieved without ambiguities. This tends to be ignored in documents which appear totally to reject present structures, and demand entirely new ones, with only the vaguest indication of what they should embody, or of the process of change.

3. *Study*: Careful and trained reasoning on the basis of specialized knowledge must not be thought of as elitist. For

example, it was trained biological and earth scientists who first brought ecological issues to the attention of the WCC. And even on their own ground, so to speak, the churches need skilled help in biblical and theological studies, and in elucidating how to move from them to decision making in personal and social ethics.

I mention a few issues that need disciplined work: the place and use of Just War criteria (already mentioned); the status of the nation as a political entity (uncritically assumed in WCC documents); the ethics of risk taking; problems of democratic processes in plural societies. And as far as the remit of the WCC is concerned, underlying all its social ethics is the balance between its educational and consultative role and its activist one. This governs all I have discussed so far, and all that is to come.

5 The Church and its Function in Society

The title of this chapter is that of the book by W. A. Visser't Hooft and J. H. Oldham which, as I mentioned in chapter 1, was sent to all the participants in the Oxford Conference of 1937 one month beforehand. It remains a classic. Such a title could cover a study of the entire phenomenon of Christianity in its history and its global context today, but in this chapter it is directed towards a reflection on what is at the heart of the life of the church, and how that can best be expressed in corporate decisions by churches on current issues; and how they can best help individual Christians make decisions as citizens on such issues, whether in their jobs or their families or in civic life.

1. Worship, thought and action

(a) Worship

There is a saying of Reinhold Niebuhr to the effect that the only time the church is really sufferable is when she is at prayer, for when she talks she claims too much for herself. Even this is an overstatement, because it is possible for worship itself to be corrupted and become a means of promoting self-esteem. There is the story of the worshipper who came out of a church in Leeds one Sunday morning and said he had just listened to the finest prayer ever addressed to a Leeds congregation. We know what was meant. We all must have had similar experiences, from the sermon, maybe, and not only from prayers. Yet the author of the vast study of French spirituality, H. Brémond, said in the early years of this century 'worship disinfects conduct from egoism'. At the heart of worship is praise. We are responding to good news of God made known to us through Jesus Christ and the church which resulted from his ministry. We respond with praise. It is a bit like coming upon a spectacular view when out walking, cycling or motoring and stopping simply to say 'How splendid!'. Praise takes us out of ourselves and sets us within larger horizons and deeper visions of goodness. It is these deeper visions which challenge us to express them in our lives. And it is in the light of them that we realize the gulf between our vision and our achievements, between what ought to be the case and what is in fact the case with us. There is a splendid sentence in the General Confession in the *Book of Common Prayer* of the Church of England which expresses this. 'We have left undone those things which we ought to have done; And we have done those things which we ought not to have done.' Yet the same gospel which has led us to praise and then to confession, leads us further into a renewed path of joyful – and thoughtful – obedience on our pilgrim way. It is indeed possible to twist Christian worship into subtle, or even at times blatant, forms of self-esteem, but it is not easy to corrupt. That is why it can be said that it 'disinfects conduct from egoism'. That is why it is the fundamental activity of the church.

The church has many things it ought to do, and worship which bears no relation to what we do in the many hours we are not worshipping together, is an abomination. The corruption of the best is the worst, as the Latin tag says. But all the other activities in which churches and their members may get involved are also, in the bundle of humanity in which we are placed, being engaged in by others; whereas no other body can engage in Christian worship except the church. It is made up of those who have had the good fortune to have heard of the gospel and responded to it, and cannot but see that a response of praise for what we have freely received is called for. If the church fails here it fails at the heart of its life.

However, worship is both a spur to thought and action and a prop to sustain them. No one is so strong in faith as not to need a challenge, and not to need consolation in the tangles of human living. The intimate sides of human life and also the public side, where an effort must be made to work for a more human and less unjust world, can be hard going, and we can meet with many disappointments and rebuffs. We need one another, different as we all are, with differing views in our approaches to the world and, indeed, to the many sides of the gospel, to encourage and learn from one another, within the context of our common praise.

(b) Thought

Just as Christian faith always seeks understanding, and is always reflecting on the meaning of what it has inherited from the past in the light of ever-changing cultural and intellectual settings in the present, so it is continually seeking an appropriate expression in public and private life. Faith and Order must always go together with Life and Work. The fundamental option of faith can be simple, but that does not mean an unexamined faith, nor the absence within the Christian community of efforts to foster the mutual growth of every member to their full stature in Christ.

This is the reason for a stress on the laity, and the effort to free the churches from the overwhelmingly clerical domination from which nearly all of them have suffered. The formation of a thoughtful laity is of fundamental importance.

Lay folk can worship together, including listening to hundreds of sermons, without getting an informed grip on matters of faith and life. They need help in becoming articulate, and active. Private prayer and reading are part of this process of formation, but for most people the experience of becoming articulate and learning from the experience of others, whilst contributing their own, involves some kind of group study and discussion. This usually requires a sensitive leader who facilitates but does not dominate. Laity have to give some time to such groups, apart from that spent in public worship and, probably, the part they play in keeping the structures of congregational life, including its finances and buildings, in good shape.

Groups can be of all kinds, on various levels of difficulty, and with many possible agendas. Some can be based on one congregation; others can be drawn from several congregations from the same confessional tradition; some can be ecumenical, and the more of these the better. Some can be on an occupational basis. Churches have done something on these lines for teachers and those engaged in education; to a lesser extent for those in the medical and para-medical professions; and to some extent with those in industry through the development of Urban and Industrial Mission. But there are many areas of life where little has been done – administration and the arts, to give two examples. Such groups are likely to be wider than one congregation or even one area.

Moreover they can often gain by having as members some who are not Christians, but share a common concern with Christians, and are willing to join with them in a common enquiry

Groups such as these, in addition to drawing upon the experience of their members, often need study materials, and sometimes study guides issued in connection with them. Here the reports of such bodies as Boards for Social Responsibility come in. Here also the WCC in many areas can call on resources wider in reference and depth than can national or local bodies. What is needed is a sifting of the mass of evidence on 'what is going on', assessing the more significant data amongst it, and also the most plausible reactions to it, together with drawing attention to theological issues that are raised, and the queries advocates of each plausible reaction put to the advocates of the others. If the data are not handled well, but in ways which are too simple, by accepting some interpretations uncritically through ignoring contrary evidence, taking always the worst possible case analysis, or operating within a theological basis which may be unavowed but, if stated, is queried by many thoughtful Christians, those responsible fail in the very task they have set out to discharge. The WCC has to guard against this.

It is obvious that such groups must be able to cope with internal conflicts of opinion, which can be sharp, without splitting up in disorder, a point I shall return to shortly. It is also clear that in so far as Christians must hope that others will come to share in the good news of the gospel, it is out of such an openness of worship and thought, combined with an effort to increase a ministry in the world which goes beyond thought to action, which is designed to promote justice, mercy and reconciliation, that others can best be drawn to it.

(c) Action

Actions which go beyond dealing with relief work caused by wars and natural disasters are almost always controversial. The Programme to Combat Racism has been a good example. Individual Christians can, and may be expected to, act personally as citizens through political parties, trade unions and professional associations, and pressure groups (whether single- or multi-issue).

One thinks, for example, of Help the Aged, Shelter (concerned with the homeless), the Child Poverty Action Group, environmental protests when proposed new motorways threaten to destroy stretches of countryside or wild life habitats, or a traffic congestion threatened by the siting of a hypermarket. Or, again, Christians can combine with other Christians in their own pressure groups, like Church Action on Poverty, or Christian Pacifist or Christian Socialist groups. Or they may engage in symbolic actions to arouse public concern about, to quote examples, homelessness or political oppressions and tyranny.

I am more concerned at the moment with official action by representative bodies such as Synods or Assemblies. Thought should lead to action. Action often begins with words in the shape of criticisms of current ideas and practices. This is usually thought of as the prophetic office of the church. I shall consider this in chapter 8. It may include prophetic action, such as the creation of special funds for compaigns or projects, like the Ecumenical Development Co-operative Society (based in Holland). This is activity in the socio-political realms. 'Political' is not being used here in the narrower sense of party politics, for it would be rare indeed in most parts of the world for the church to identify itself with one political party. If it has had any tendency to do so it has been on nationalist lines, not a happy precedent. But most public issues are political in the broad sense. To achieve anything (except under military governments) it has to be achieved through politicians, who in turn have to work in relation to party machinery. Sometimes issues arise which cut across party divisions, like the question of Sunday trading in Britain. But all these issues are contentious. Opinions will differ. The evidence will be incomplete, or unclear and open to more than one interpretation. The trade-offs involved in pursuing particular policies are likely to be in dispute and evaluated differently. Church people are often afraid to engage on any such issues because they cause controversy. They fear splits in the congregation, or the Synods, or whatever. The fellowship will be impaired or broken. Dissenters may walk out in annoyance.

This fear goes to the root of the nature and quality of the fellowship (*koinonia*) that binds Christians and churches together. If there is a reluctance to take up any current issue for fear of controversy, the Christian community is compelled to be on the sidelines on issues on which responsible citizens must engage. In that case is not their worship escapist? More than that, to do nothing about issues is to acquiesce in things as they are; and to do so irresponsibly by neglect rather than by thought and deliberate decisions. And to do that is itself to makes a political judgment. Further still, churches (and to a lesser extent individuals), by their ownership of property, savings and investment funds, are inevitably active in the political realm. Politics is a sea in which it is impossible not to swim. Churches are not organized primarily for this; primarily they are organized for worship; but they have to learn how to deal with political issues, by promoting alertness, handling discussions, and holding together those who choose different policies and ensuring that they keep in dialogue with fellow Christians as they do so.

The activity most people think of when church leaders, Synods, Assemblies and conferences are in mind, is the passing of resolutions. These can indeed be educative and influential if well worked for, but they can also be ephemeral, unrepresentative and a waste of time. J. H. Oldham remarks that before resolutions are passed it should be clear who is precisely committed to do what by them.[1] Otherwise they give those who pass them the illusion of having done something significant when in fact it has been a matter of empty words. It is too easy.

A related point is that when ordained church leaders or representative bodies do make pronouncements or pass resolutions, their weight depends upon the weight of the briefing behind them. If not well briefed, silence is better than something ill-considered or platitudinous. This applies to the laity and the ordained alike. J. H. Oldham in an article in 1960 in the journal *Frontier* (since defunct), wrote, 'The crucial point is not the distinction between laity and clergy, but the question of competence in the various spheres of secular activity.' He denied 'the assumption that to be a Christian gives a man superiority over his fellows in the decision of questions that call for technical knowledge or for painfully won wisdom in dealing with practical affairs.' This is not entirely adequate, because there are occasions in some disciplines when what is thought to be purely technical disguises assumptions about human beings and their world which is not technical but ideological. In that case a theological critique is needed, to consider whether the view is consonant with a Christian view, or is akin to it but based on the presuppositions of a different religion or philosophy, or is 'secular' in the bad sense of the word. The social sciences are more liable to this than the natural sciences, but the latter have also to be watched. Nevertheless, Oldham's warning is broadly salutary.

Producing a well-informed laity is more important than passing resolutions. Such laity will be able to live with the inevitable uncertainties in making ethical decisions; decisions which often cannot be put off until some future time when it is hoped the evidence will be clearer. They are ventures of faith. We need to be delivered from expecting a clear 'Christian' line on most of the decisions we are called upon to make. Action is in the context of faith, not sight. We learn greater discernment from the lessons of experience.

2. *The church as mystery and human institution*

'Mystery' in the New Testament can be popularly translated as 'open secret'. A reality has been disclosed, not to a select few who need some esoteric knowledge to understand it, but in principle to everyone. But it is a reality which points to more than it is able fully to express in words or in actions. For that reason it is beyond what sociological categories can fully capture, even though it is not exempt from their categorization. It is a mystery.

The New Testament claims that a new kind of fellowship (*koinonia*) has come into existence as a gift of God through the ministry of Jesus the Christ; a barrier breaking fellowship. In it barriers between Jew and Gentile, free and slave, men and women, are overcome. The fact that this reality was known in their own experience and accepted in principle by church members is shown by St Paul's letters. When he is rebuking quarrelling Christians in the churches to which he writes, his chief weapon is an appeal to what he knows they know to be the case. They are fouling their own nests. They are negating the gift of the new community they have received in Christ.

The church is not just an advance model of a modern 'western' political democracy, nor a replica of an hierarchical political

structure from the past. The *sensus fidelium*, the common understanding by church members of their faith, is more elusive than
either of these political models, and is always on the way to being
realized rather than a static achievement.

At the same time the church *is* a human structure. It is not
exempt from an examination drawn from socio-political
categories and management studies, though they themselves must
be seen to have some indeterminacy, and are not to be thought
of as 'laws' in a narrow sense. The structure of the WCC is a
'system', as I have mentioned in chapter 3. Occasional ecumenical
attention is paid to these matters, usually under the heading of
'non-theological' factors hindering Christian unity. If it means
factors which ecclesiologists in Faith and Order often ignore, the
term is correct; though in a broad sense they often have a theological element which needs a theological critique.[2] An example of
a more clearly non-theological factor is the level of taxation,
particularly income and inheritance taxes. In 'western' societies
modern rates of taxation have hindered the fissiparousness of
Protestantism, where the classic pattern has been the breakaway
of a dissident minority to form a new church, largely financed by a
few wealthy laity.

Sociological theory has difficulty in coping with a church structure which is composed of a committed core at the centre of a
congregation, combined with an open policy on the fringes. The
typological division into church and sect is too neat. Sects have had
more attention because they are smaller and more clearly typified.
Churches, and denominations as a kind of uneasy sub-division of
them, are less easy. However, one socio-political 'law', that of 'the
iron law of oligarchy' certainly has some bearing on them. It says
that under the semblance of democracy real power lies with the
energetic few, because of the apathy of the majority, or their
incoherence. At the Canberra Assembly of the WCC it was not
apathy which bedeviled the 'business' side of it, but the incoherent
innocence of those present. I return to this in the final section.

It is necessary to examine how church structures actually work
in terms of power, and not take their self-definition for granted.[3]
For instance an aura of holiness can disguise a denial in practice of
natural justice.[4] The church cannot claim a total sociological
uniqueness. Its mystery is partly, though not exclusively, mediated

through its ordinariness. Its structures bear, within the element of *koinonia* which underlies them, a 'family resemblance' (to use a phrase made familiar by the philosophy of Wittgenstein), to other social and political structures.

Management theory uses the language of cybernetics, and the concepts of a system, and feed back, as I have mentioned in chapter 3. Five types of management theory are sometimes differentiated: (1) Traditional, which is patriarchal and reflects the hierarchical nature of traditional societies; (2) Charismatic, which is intuitive and more the product of the individualistic and buccaneering spirit of nineteenth-century industrial capitalism; (3) Classical, often called rational or bureaucratic, reflecting the work of more 'scientific' management studies, what Max Weber called 'the routinization of charisma'; as industry settled down to more steady development, units grew in size, and management became more complex. (4) Human relations style of management, reflecting the influence of developmental psychology (as in the work of A.H. Maslow and others), and the desire to give capitalism a more human face. (5) Systemic management, which is an open system, responding to changes in the outside world, and in which leaders are monitored as they look outwards, beyond the organization, as much as inwards.

Those who produce such analyses tend to favour the fifth. Applied to the church the emphasis on looking outwards and monitoring the leaders have far-reaching implications. There are signs of its influence. Bishops, clergy and ministers are beginning gingerly some experiments on internal appraisal of their work. Probably all five elements have a place in church structures, but the effort to look at them in this perspective is in its early days. It could have a considerable effect on the WCC.[5]

3. *The WCC: A major case study*

Since most of this book is concerned with the WCC the two case studies which now follow can be relatively brief. Their aim is to look at the nature of the WCC, and two of its recent activities, the Canberra Assembly and the Seoul Convocation, with the background of the discussion in this chapter of the church and its function in society in mind.

The WCC is unique in its origin, task and destiny. It is as the Christian church itself. Its task arises from the disunity of that church and its need for renewal. Its destiny is to make itself unnecessary. But it is still subject to socio-political and management analysis. As a mystery it is a conciliar fellowship or, more accurately, a pre-conciliar fellowship. As we have seen, the Toronto Statement of 1950 has never been amended, and yet it plainly does not entirely correspond to the reality. The churches find it hard to verbalize the reality which holds them together, as they learn more of one another, and from one another in their common worship and dialogue, so different from the indifference and hostility of the past. The WCC is complex. It is global. It spans the Catholic-Protestant division (as to a lesser extent the Orthodox and Anglicans do). Its inner life is a mystery.

How can it combine representativeness and competence? It has met the full force of the urgency of the Third World, now at last getting a hearing. Those who have been hurt most, and felt it for a long time, are now present in large numbers and vocal. They are being heard. However, a sense of hurt can often cloud the judgment and lead to misinterpretations and over-simplified analyses. Every perspective is partial and needs exposure to other perspectives. At the moment, as already mentioned, the 'western liberals' have a sense of guilt, and are inhibited from making a necessary contribution from their own background.

Structurally there have been at the WCC too many 'desks', inclined to develop their own interests. Quality of work suffers. There is a danger of general mediocrity. A slimming of the agenda is called for. Also more varied expert evidence needs to be brought in and, of course, to be sifted. This will not override a 'preferential option for the poor', but it will guard against uncritically accepting slogans, and proposals which might in fact harm them.

As an instrument of unity and renewal the WCC must not merely be an instrument of the present perception by the churches of their mission and their interests. It needs to challenge them. This is not easy for churches to accept. It is not only the Roman Catholic authorities who find this difficult. Yet the WCC (and national councils of churches) have to guard against never moving beyond what is unanimously agreed, lest the whole enterprise is put at the mercy of the least open and least resilient. It has to tread the difficult path of holding together those who disagree at some points by reminding all members of at least the elements of a true church which they recognize in others. There will always be tensions here until the WCC has succeeded in making itself redundant.

It is true that the Ecumenical Movement is wider than the WCC, but it remains for the present a vital framework and support for it. However, institutional inflexibility on the part of the churches leads the WCC to look beyond their official structures. Konrad Raiser, now its General Secretary, has stressed the creativity of covenant communities among minorities within the churches.[6] Their lack of institutional power is their strength; as local, informal structures they reveal the oppressive claims of all universal projects. There is truth here, but dangers too. Their creativity is a challenge, but their absence of power greatly diminishes their relevance in dealing with the power structures of the churches. Also these power structures are felt at local levels. Even there the WCC cannot avoid them. And they are much stronger centrally. Concentration on the local can be a 'small is beautiful' romanticism, and an escape from working away at undermining entrenched rigidities.

4. *Canberra and Seoul: A minor case study*

As at Vancouver the aim was that Canberra should be a thoroughly participatory Assembly. In worship it achieved this, with little to say to the contrary, except perhaps than an element of populism in it encouraged simplistic thought. In other ways the production of reports and, above all, the business side of the ultimate organ of authority for the WCC, were both hampered.

Large numbers of delegates were inexperienced, many at their first major ecumenical event. They had little or no knowledge of the heritage of ecumenical thinking. The very size of the occasion, a tribute to the success of the WCC, was bewildering. It was made worse by the general mixing for much of the time of delegates with the large numbers of observers and visitors. Plenary sessions easily became chaotic. Determined individuals, some of them advocates of special interest groups, could get something inserted in a report if it was said with passion. Some were inclined to push a private agenda rather than that of the church which sent them. A prime example of confusion was an amendment proposed by Konrad Raiser calling on the churches to give up any theological or moral justification for the use of military power, which was passed one day and rescinded the next, when its implications were realized. There was no sense of a tradition of theological thought in this area.

Final draft statements were not available until the last day, so the Assembly was bold in even commending the substance of them. Included in them was a condemnation of the International Monetary Fund, the World Bank, the General Agreement on Trade and Tariffs, and the power of the market system! The drafts were made up from the work of sections and sub-sections. The leaders of many of these were unprepared and inadequate, and some of the rapporteurs and Moderators of sections were inexperienced. The early preparatory materials for sections 1 and 2 were a collection of previous WCC statements, and a booklet prepared unofficially by three people and open to some serious criticisms.[7] In fact it was only distributed at the Assembly itself, and could hardly have even been skimmed through there. The Assembly lacked the experience of those involved in public affairs, or engaged in administrative and managerial responsibility (except for the formal visit of the Australian Prime Minister).

These features have not been unknown before in major WCC events, but they seem to have reached a new intensity at Canberra. Four days were cut from the previous Assembly at Vancouver, on grounds of cost, but there was no cut in the agenda. The sense of confusion and lack of mutual trust was shown in the process of selecting the Central Committee by bemused and jejune delegates. In a radio interview, a leading church person said of the process – 'it stinks'.

The conclusion of Professor Horsbrugh of Sydney University is that 'Assemblies like this cannot continue'. It becomes essential to distinguish between something like the huge *Kirchentag*, which the Evangelical (Lutheran) and Roman Catholic churches each hold every alternate year in Germany, and an Assembly of the WCC; and between that and a study conference or consultation. The Seoul Convocation of 1990 is an example of the latter.

It was another instance of confusion. It illustrates the need for careful preparatory work and timetabling. The possibility of preparatory work being modified or rejected must, of course, be allowed for. No false unanimity is to be sought. Only by good preparatory material could hundreds of delegates reasonably deal with the agenda in the time available, or reach conclusions which would provide substantial guidelines for the WCC into the next millennium. Instead there was confusion between fundamental policy recommendations, and specific policies. This is a familiar story, but Seoul was an extreme example. Some of the grass roots organizations, some of them non-church, opposed the mainline churches. There was a persistent tendency to advance particular actions on social, economic and political issues as part of the definition of a church, an error I discussed in the previous chapter. The proceedings were so chaotic that no agreed reports could be issued. The experts present were not called on, and listened helplessly.

Four agreed Commitments and ten Affirmations emerged, and even these on examination have several questionable features.

I mention first the four Commitments.

1. To a just economic order, and to no burden of foreign debt. One can hardly be in favour of injustice, the problem is to flush out the criteria of justice, a notorious difficulty. No one can be in favour of bondage; the problem is to flush out how foreign debts are to be handled. Or are they to be shunned? In that case governments will have to impose a fearful burden of forced savings on their citizens.

2. To security for all nations and a culture of non-violence. This takes the basic status of the nation-state for granted, a very dubious assumption. Also violence is the term we use for the use of force in situations when we do not consider it justified. The need is to be as clear as possible when force is legitimate and necessary. Or are we committed to abjuring force completely? That would indeed be utopia.

3. To a culture in harmony with nature's integrity. This takes over as clear a phrase which has recently come into vogue in the WCC, but which is far from clear. I discuss this in the next chapters.

4. To the eradication of racism. This *is* reasonably clear, in that the concept of racism is now widely understood.

Seoul added ten Affirmations.

1. All exercise of power is accountable to God. This is church language. We also have to think out how secular governments and international agencies are to regard their accountability and be held to it. A similar comment on the need to relate Christian affirmations to secular ones occurs in relation to most of the following Affirmations.

2. God's option for the poor.

3. The equal value of all races and peoples. The use of the dubious term 'race' is unfortunate.

4. Male and female as made in God's image.

5. Truth is the foundation of the community of free peoples. One wonders how far there can be exclusive or complete claims to possess it.

6. The peace of Jesus Christ. One asks how the Peace in the title of the Convocation (Justice, Peace and the Integrity of Creation) relates to the eschatological peace of Jesus 'which passes all understanding'.

7. The creation as beloved of God. In affirming this one asks how, in biblical terms, this stress, from Genesis 1 and 2, is related to that on 'the Fall' in Genesis 3?

8. The earth is the Lord's.

9. The dignity and commitment of the younger generation. This is bizarre. The younger generation is no more free from 'Original Sin' than the older. The young have their own characteristic temptations, such as to take up dangerous causes promoted by facile slogans; the old are tempted to acquiesce too easily in familiar evils.

10. Human rights are given by God. But so are human responsibilities; there is no mention of these.

Altogether this is a meagre harvest from a long-heralded but inadequately prepared and badly run global consultation. The WCC cannot afford a repetition of anything like it. It is no help in illuminating the functions of the church in society.

The work of the Oxford Conference was ahead of the thought of the churches, and indeed of secular thought, in the 1930s. That is not true of the work of the WCC now, which has been in decline since Vancouver. It has tied itself too closely to simplistic theological and ideological critiques of the contemporary world, and has failed to recognize how political and economic changes have undermined them. It is not the help to the churches that it ought to be, and there is a loss of confidence in organized ecumenism.[8]

Part Two

Present and Future

6 Where We are Today
1: Three Issues

The three issues discussed in this chapter are clearly pressing ones in the 1990s. Not surprisingly they have been given a good deal of attention by the WCC. My purpose in outlining my own approach to them is to illustrate a perspective which I think has hardly been represented in the WCC work on them. There are other important issues which are part of the ecumenical horizon with which I do not deal; the role of nationalism, the legitimacy of the nation-state, the control and use of force in civil strife, war and revolutionary struggles, and racism as an exacerbating factor in all of them. This is to mention a few. I add a note on them.[1] But I do not deal with them, partly because the three chosen are ones where the WCC has published most in recent years.

1. *Problems created by the collapse of the Soviet system*

This collapse was as complete as it was unexpected. In 1989 no one was foreseeing it. The collapse led to a certain nostalgia among many, Christians included, both overt and covert, and reflected in many WCC documents, because of the distrust of competition, profits, and the free market as the heir to the central-ized Soviet-style economy; and also because it did seem to guarantee the basics of life – food, housing, health care, education and employment – to all citizens. There was, of course, no approval of the amount of political repression and the power of *apparatchiks* which went with this, in so far as it was realized, but the idea lurked that, freed from these distortions, hidden in the Marxist theories is an economically effective and politically just way of running the social order. This is an illusion. There has been no serious ecumenical analysis of the ethical and ideological consequences of the collapse of Soviet-style socialism. The end of it and of the Cold War appear to be regretted in some WCC documents because they are assumed to be seen as the triumph of 'western' capitalism; and because it means a unipolar world without countervailing power to that of the USA, the globalization of international capital, and the promotion of the free market as a miracle cure for all economic ills.

The economic failure was on a colossal scale, both in quantity as well as the quality of goods and services produced. So was the pollution it created. Only in arms production and space exploration did the USSR have notable achievements, and the economic cost of these was very great in the amount of forced savings imposed on the consumer by the absence of consumer goods in the shops, a deprivation so great that no government which had to face genuinely free elections could have imposed it. Marxism does not provide a third way of running an economy between a centralized and a market model; neither for that matter does Roman Catholic social teaching, for that claim is abandoned in the latest Papal social Encyclical, *Centesimus Annus*.

A move from a centralized to a market economy is a rough one. There are no precedents to go on. The laisser-faire ideology of the market economy, the polar opposite to that of the centralized one, is a mirage. In 'western' terminology some form of social market or democratic socialist economy is called for.[2] Ex-communist countries in eastern Europe had begun a reform on these lines before the collapse of the USSR, but on the whole they had failed. They started from different bases. Polish farms, for instance, had never been collectivized. Hungary had gone furthest. But they had tried to reform parts of the system leaving the rest untouched. The central fixing of prices remained, and this meant that supplies fell off. Queues lengthened. Inflation began. Yet the problem for more democratic governments of surviving the shock of attending to everything at once is formidable (witness Poland's 'big bang' in 1990). It involves letting market prices be established, the abandonment of subsidies to loss-making state enterprises, dismantling trade barriers, being open to foreign competition, and attracting domestic and foreign investment. (The Comecon trade system collapsed in 1991 when Russia moved to trading in hard currency.) It involves the erection of an institutional framework of a market economy; laws of contract and ownership, and a new tax system. Half-heartedness in doing this runs the danger of the hyper-inflation which rocked the German social structure in 1922–23. So far unemployment has soared as dynamism produces social dislocation; and economic greed and corruption has replaced political corruption as the problem. But there are goods in the shops!

Keynes once remarked that the aim of the economic and political order should be efficiency (in the use of relatively scarce resources), social justice and liberty. What sort of mix between them do we need now? Even in Beijing the *People's Daily* on 23 February 1992, after praising capitalism's historic role, can be found calling for 'adequately developing the capitalist economy inside China'. In 1991 Chinese Gross National Product grew by 7% in real terms, and in the coastal regions by over 10%. But Deng Xiaoping wants to absorb the economic ideas of capitalism and combine them with strict political control. Pinochet in Chile wanted to do the same. In the long run it will not work. Neither China nor Russia will be able to sustain a market economy with a move to, or a retaining of, political authoritarianism.

The market as the sole economic tool has serious defects, even though we can pass by the rhetoric of the Vancouver Assembly of the WCC that it is the product of 'satanic forces'. The problem is to attend to its defects without destroying its essential mechanisms or liberal social democratic virtues. It is easy to criticize liberalism as an ideology, and it has become a target for many contemporary philosophers and theologians, who run the danger of cutting off the bough on which they sit. In any case liberal institutions are a different matter. It is worth noting that Roman Catholic social teaching continues to criticize liberalism as an ideology whilst coming gradually to accept liberal institutions.

Public ownership is no longer seen as the key issue (though the British Labour Party has still not had the realism to remove it from Clause 4 of its Constitution). Nor is a simple opposition between capital and labour the right focus. Rather it is that between the employed and the unemployed, the skilled and the unskilled, and the bias against ethnic minorities and one parent families. The root issue is how to help all those adversely affected by dynamic change, not leaving them to the unmerciful forces of the market. There is the even more basic question, Do we want dynamic change; or do we want to preserve stability? The attitude of many Christians seems to favour stability. I shall return to this.

Let us briefly assess the market, morally, economically and politically. Morally there is no reason to question competition, profit and self interest (properly understood), and much to commend them in the freedom and responsibility that go with them. The moral objection to the market is that, left to itself, it treats labour, which is intimately bound up with the integrity of the person, as a factor of production having no more status than land and capital, which are not so intimately bound up with it. Also the virtues of the market have been much exaggerated. It presupposes basic moral virtues which it does not promote, often ignores, and in practice may undermine. It has no place for equality as an economic and social criterion and, because of the inequalities of income and inheritance it encourages, it has difficulty even in maintaining equality before the law. Wealth gives power.

Economically, a free market does enable us to maximize the output of our relatively scarce resources; that is why it is dynamic. This is important because most of us are divided creatures who want dynamism in theory so long as we are not disturbed in our niche in the economy. Nevertheless there are other values which always have to be considered and which modify the sole pursuit of efficiency in the economic sense. Inequalities of wealth, often due to luck more than meritorious dynamism, distort the market so that the wealthy can command luxuries whilst the poor have not the purchasing power to command necessities. The market is also defective in many areas. It cannot in practice look ahead more than ten to fifteen years. Many issues of public policy – transport and environmental issues among them – need a longer perspective, hazardous as it may be to forecast. Nor can the market deal with collective requirements like defence, public spaces and town planning, nor with 'externalities', that is to say the accompanying cost to the community of economic operations which the producer does not pay. Many pollution issues are instances of this.

Politically, economic power is related to political power. To some extent the market is a liberation in this respect, unless it is undermined by monopolies or oligopolies (where there are very few producers), against which vigilance is always needed. Similarly the GATT (General Agreement on Trade and Tariffs) issues are in a liberalizing direction. I shall say more about this in the next section. But the greater economic and political power of the capitalist world and, in the past, of the Soviet one, has pressed hardly on the Third World. How to empower it is a key question. Should economic growth in the First World be stopped in favour of the Third? Can it be? Is the world of international trade a zero sum game? I shall also return to this.

Considerations of economic and political power run into one another, and there are always trade-offs between them. For instance professional bodies by their regulatory practices protect the consumer from rogues and charlatans; on the other hand they can put the profession into a position of power which exposure to the market can diminish. On the other hand it may be easy in the market to get away with sharp practice; consumers need protection. Merely saying *caveat emptor* (let the buyer beware) is not enough. An *ombudsman* is needed. Politically, the law should protect the citizen against the misuse of power in the market, by professional bodies, and by the State itself.[3]

To return to Keynes and his triad of efficiency, liberty and social justice. No sharp line between social, economic, civil and political freedom can be drawn. Freedom is more than freedom from coercion, or freedom to do what one likes. Those who argue, like Hayek,[4] that poverty is not unfreedom because no one is politically prevented from any action by poverty, ought to realize that lack of access to resources to what the majority of citizens are free to do, is a lack of freedom. Those who want to make a sharp division between the two say that civil and political freedoms can be clearly defined, whereas social and economic ones are open-ended and insatiable as, for instance, the demand for health care. But as the working of legal rights can be scrutinized and made more effective, so can socio-economic ones. The fact that they cannot be totally instantiated need not prevent an ongoing public debate on how they can be better instantiated; that is to say on the fairness with which relatively scarce resources are allocated in both areas.[5]

What recent contribution has the WCC made to these issues? The Canberra Assembly, at the time of the crumbling of the Soviet system, paid little attention to it. Instead it criticized the World Bank, the International Monetary Fund and GATT, and said the market system needed reform, if not transformation. Of course it needs reform. One can say of it *semper reformanda* (always in need of reform), as one can of the church, and of the WCC itself. The free market is an 'ideal' concept, always in search of a better realization. But transformation? Into what? No clue is given. A booklet 'The Political Economy of the Holy Spirit', distributed to Sections 1 and 2 at Canberra says, 'The most invidious false spirit today is the power of the market.'[6]

In this area the last production of the former Commission of the Churches on Participation in Development, on which a good deal of trouble was taken, is 'Christian Faith and the World Economy Today'.[7] It strikes different notes, and parts of it are acute. But there are elements of unreality in its analysis which need to be noted. It does not clearly spell out the significance of the collapse of the Soviet-style economies, and that there is no alternative on offer other than some variant of the market economy. It tends to stress the disadvantages of the market, and to continue the old Christian socialist demand for co-operation, not competition. It talks of new patterns of ownership, without specifying them, and shows some suspicion of international trade, and of export-led growth. It makes the basic error of saying of international trade that 'unless carried out by equals it leads to impoverishment', which treats it as a zero sum game, that the wealth of one state is the poverty of another – the eighteenth-century mercantilist fallacy. By demanding the cancellation of Third World debts it does not consider the level of forced savings governments would have to levy on their citizens if they cannot borrow internationally. It does not seem clear on whether dynamism is desirable. By endorsing the cause of western European small farmers, and aboriginal land claims, it appears to favour the preservation of both as economic entities – a static option. There is a serious problem here, but it needs further exploration. It rails against an unequal world, but how precisely are we to cope with an unequal endowment between nation-states in terms of natural resources? Since these cannot be changed, what other factors can be brought in? However, natural resources are not the only factor. Hong Kong and Singapore prosper with scarcely any.

Education can be more important, especially the education of girls. Politically, the booklet takes nation-states for granted and calls for a greater UN effort to correct the imbalance of power between them. But the UN and its agencies reflect this imbalance, and the Security Council is constructed to express it. International power cannot be abolished. The crucial question is, How far can a cogent self-interest argument be mounted to induce more economic and political power sharing by the First World? The Brandt Commission argues on those lines, but it has not had much effect.[8]

I have no clear answer to these questions, but I would hope for a sharper analysis of them and a clearer focus from the WCC than it has so far provided, a concern which will be further explored in the next section.

2. *Economic growth and sustainability in a global context*

The Bruntland Report of 1987 called for 'sustainable development', involving a 3% per annum rise in income per head; that is to say continued growth, but at a slower rate than was the case.[9] It urged greater production with the use of fewer resources through greater efficiency and through recycling. It looked for a reduction in the probable population explosion; and a redistribution from the areas of affluent over-consumption to those of poorer under-consumers.

Some dismissed this as 'patent nonsense'. The critics said the Commission fudged the main issue, which is development without growth because the limits to growth have already been reached. More pollution is being created than even that great sink, the oceans, can absorb, and more non-renewable resources are being used than can be replaced by alternatives. Also by the time the evidence of the 'greenhouse effect' has become irrefutable it will be too late to avert it. A cautiously pessimistic policy is called for, as the irreversible effects of an optimistic one would be too serious. So there is the call for a 'steady state' economy, with negative growth for the rich countries, the necessity of avoiding wastefulness, and the demand for an energy conservation body, like the International Atomic Energy Agency. In this paragraph I have quoted from an UNESCO booklet written with the Rio de Janeiro summit of 1992 in mind.[10] Although it is published by

UNESCO three of its authors are, or were, Advisers to the
Environmental Department of the World Bank. The bank clearly
did not embrace it, for it hired an independent team of economists
who took a different line in the bank's World Development
Report of 1992, 'Development and the Environment'. This report
said that the cure for poverty is economic growth, provided it
takes proper account of environmental costs. This includes proper
pricing policies for water, electricity, and timber, by removing
subsidies on them, together with good administration to operate
regulations which are realistically enforceable. It said that if
developing countries spent 1.5% of their Gross Domestic Product
on this it would be enough. It also said that the best long-term
environmental policy is the better education of girls. Those with
secondary education have an average of three children, those with
only primary education have seven. Moreover it urged that the
rich countries, worried about the greenhouse effect and the reduction of biological diversity, should pay poor countries to carry out
restrictive measures beyond their immediate national interests. But
it maintained that a clean water policy and one guarding against
soil erosion are more important than problems of global warming.

Before reflecting further on the debate between steady state and
sustainable development it is important not to be complacent
about the seriousness of the issue. The UN Human Development
Programme for its 1992 Human Development Report pointed
out that the gap between the richer 20% of the world and the
poorer 20% has doubled since 1960. (This of course is a relative
comparison and does not deal with absolute poverty.) Sub-Sahara
is the worst area. Moreover most aid goes to those among the
poorer countries who need it least; the richer 40% of the developing countries get double per head of the poorer 40%; and those
who spend more than 40% of their Gross Domestic Product on
armaments get double the aid per head of the more peaceable
countries. Further, the dire state of children in the Third World,
and the importance of clean water is brought out in the UNICEF
1992 Report on 'The State of the World's Children'.[11]

Returning to the question of economic growth brings us to the
question of trade. Western European countries, the USA and
Japan frustrate the trade of the Third World. In agriculture they
do it by protection of their own farmers by banning imports and

exporting their subsidized surpluses, dumping them in the Third World. In manufacturing they restrict imports by quotas, and other devices in addition to tariffs, from developing countries, (as for instance by the notorious Multi-Fibre Arrangement with respect to textiles). They do this because they want to preserve jobs in their own countries in particular industries and agriculture, ignoring or being indifferent to the extra costs this imposes on consumers in general. They do this because they will not develop dynamic social policies which would enable workers to move from those areas of the economy without undue hardship into the new areas of goods and services which a dynamic economy will develop. Rich countries, except for the Middle East oil states, also restrict labour mobility, or are highly selective in what they allow. Japan is the worst offender. Rich countries ought both to invest in developing ones and also encourage their exports. At present they receive only a ludicrous 0.2% of private investments.

It will be realized that I have tacitly come down in favour of sustainable growth rather than a steady state economy. What of the limits to growth arguments? In the long run the earth's non-renewable resources must be limited. There must also be a limit to its capacity to absorb pollution (and all human activity pollutes to some extent). But in many ways the long run is receding. The *known* resources of gas and oil are eight times larger than they were in 1980; ultimately recoverable known fossil fuel reserves are 400 times the present rate of output. What of the alleged-ecological impasse? At present it is said that humans use 40% of the terrestrial part of the earth which produces plant life. If the population were doubled twice, human activity would take 100% of it, leaving nothing for non-human species; and without them humans cannot survive. This is a matter of sifting ecological evidence, in which I have no special competence. But it is a long-range forecast. Most people would in any case agree that two doublings of the world's population would be catastrophic. Those concerned with economic growth are well aware of the need to limit population growth, as I have already mentioned in connection with the education of girls. This impasse looks like one of the Club of Rome's apocalyptic sagas. Ecologists seem prone to a kind of fundamentalism, to resist any consideration of ambiguities or trade-offs in public policies, and in particular to suspect international trade.

The case for it is widely misunderstood. Free trade is an 'ideal' concept, part of the 'ideal' free market. It shows how the world should trade *if* it wants to maximize the productivity of its relatively scarce resources. But we have seen that humans, both personally and collectively, always want to modify the market in some respects, not least because the market cannot cope with many collective problems of resource allocation, nor take a long enough view. Allowing for this, and because it is so misunderstood, it is important to understand the case for free trade.

That case argues that states should concentrate on whatever use of resources at which they are comparatively better. They may have no absolute advantage over other states in anything, but they should still concentrate on what they are comparatively best at. It is a fallacy that there is only so much output to be produced or capital to be invested, so that international trade is a zero sum game. Rather, it is a positive sum game. It raises incomes; that raises savings, which in turn raises investment and leads to a more dynamic economy. Of course there are losers as well as gainers. Social policies, as I have mentioned, are needed to help losers adjust without undue hardship. Free trade means that people must adjust to change as resources move from the now relatively unproductive uses. But means must be found of mitigating the cost of change and the consequent attachment to the *status quo* because of personal and family insecurity.

Talk of 'fair trade' instead of 'free trade', of 'creating a level playing field' is a fundamental misunderstanding, and often disguises a specious campaign by vested interests. There is a sinister alliance between some environmentalists, a few ecological economists, and employers and trade unionists (those in work ignoring those out of it), which obscures the issue. It easily develops into an 'exports good and imports bad' attitude, and hostility to international trade as such.

The book *The New Protectionism* is a good example.[12] In attacking GATT it says that jobs will flow out of Europe to countries with lower wage levels and less environmental protection. It urges that regions should produce as much of their own goods and services as they can, and that global trade should be a last resort. Aid and trade should foster local and regional self-reliance. What it ignores is that wages will rise as productivity rises, and so will standards of work and environmental protection. This does not mean that nothing should be done about sweat-shops, especially child labour, or pollution. Social policy should go along with free trade in every country.[13] Complete laisser-faire is an ideological mirage, and we have already seen that Third World countries will need assistance from the First World on environmental policies. But First World standards must not be foisted on the Third World in the name of creating a level playing field. Third World countries, who are increasingly in favour of GATT, rightly resist this.

Attitudes to GATT – now to be called the Multilateral Trade Organization – is a test case. Those who are suspicious of international trade suspect what is thought by others to be the success at the end of 1993 of the long round of Uruguay negotiations (which is where they began). It will reduce by a further one third the tariffs on industrial goods, establish the first international rules for trade in agricultural products, and in services. The Multi-Fibre Agreement, with its crippling effects on trade in textiles and clothing will be phased out; and the rules against subsidies and dumping will be strengthened. The sinister Common Agricultural Policy of the European Union will depend less on quantitative restrictions and more on tariffs and direct payments to farmers, which are more obviously open to the scrutiny of consumers, and the cost to them much clearer. There are improved safeguards for patents and copyrights. Those who are against international trade do not favour the GATT agreement, whilst many of those who do, wish it had gone further. The political problems of doing so, as governments manoeuvre to protect particular groups of their electorates, are obvious.

Those most aware of the poverty of the Third World, and knowing the weight of the power advantage of the First World, ask themselves how far the Third World will benefit from these recent GATT negotiations. The answer appears to be that, at least for a short time, the very poorest Sub-Saharan countries and some Caribbean islands will lose. They include those who have been highly dependent on privileged exports to the 'west' (for instance through the Lomé Convention, which applied to previous French colonies), and who, at the same time, are obliged to import food. This is a serious matter. Aid agencies need to do all they can to alert public opinion to shame governments into dealing specifically with the losers. But the fact that there is something to set against the gains secured by the agreement in December 1993 is not a reason for opposing it. Africa in any case is a crucial issue. At the moment it is not achieving 0.5% per annum growth, and even if it did it would take forty years to reach the level at which it was in 1975.

The World Bank has established 'poverty workshops', and issued a Poverty Reduction Handbook to its staff. Primary health care and education, revolving credit schemes to help small farmers to buy seeds, and more attention to them and rather less to the city populations, are part of what is involved.

There is much in the steady state versus sustainable growth debate which is still to be explored. It will be referred to again in the next section. There is at any rate a strong case for economic growth once it is separated from the ideology of laisser-faire. But if one reads WCC literature and reports on the theme one finds that they are full of denunciations of the market, suspicious of economic growth, and hostile to international trade. If one wanted to find guidance on the theory of international trade one could not find it. Christian theology teaches us to be aware of the self interest of persons and groups, not to find no place for it but to adopt what in other settings is called a 'hermeneutics of suspicion' in relation to it.[14] There is no examination in WCC literature of the 'unholy alliance' between those who oppose a lessening of trade barriers. For example, there are a few economists who adopt a steady state position. These are the ones the WCC favours for evidence. There is no presentation of the majority view, no setting out of the issues between them, with the inevitable ambiguities, as guidance in forming judgments. It has not served its constituency well. And the same is the case when we come in the next section and in chapter 7 to further thought on 'green' issues, and the relation of humanity to nature.

3. *Technology, humanity and the environment*

Expanding knowledge and skills expands the range of our moral concerns, personal and social, as we are called upon to make effective decisions in areas which were previously thought to be solely in the realm of providence (or 'acts of God' as the insurance industry refers to it). Behind new technical skills lies work in pure science. It takes five chemists to keep one chemical engineer going. Are these achievements too dangerous? Should we be frightened by them? Are the practitioners triumphalist? To some extent they are. Some scientists talk as if science is on the verge of producing a total explanation of the universe. This is a metaphysical or theological matter, not a scientific one. Science proceeds by abstraction and cannot encompass the whole of reality. 'Myths' are needed for that. The notion of creation is such a myth. Also in the advance of science and technology questions of personal career ambitions, group rivalry, commercial advantage, and national prestige all enter in and require critical scrutiny. They are perhaps most obvious in the largest enterprises such as space exploration, or the pursuit of nuclear fusion as an energy source; the former uses existing technology, the latter will require one which does not yet exist.

Clearly not everything which can be done should be done. How is it possible to differentiate between them and control the advance of science and technology? The nearer they come to personal life the less sure are human beings about their success. Genetic therapy sounds promising, but talk of genetic engineering is another matter. It conjures up alarming possibilities. When Dietrich Bonhoeffer wrote of man come of age[15] he was not thinking of moral maturity (as some persistently interpret him), but of the great areas of decision making which human beings, under God, have acquired in the dynamic modern world. It was a call to have the courage to take responsibility. What if we are able to choose the sex of our children, or to produce a genetical clone of ourselves? (It would not be identical with us because nurture would be different from nature, in that the social and cultural milieu would have changed.) These are possibilities on the horizon.

New problems connected with issues of life and death are with us now. Should we use foetal material in *in vitro* fertilization?[16] How do we assess the status of a patient in a permanently vegetative state? These are but two examples. Questions of method in making moral distinctions will be treated in chapter 8, but it can be said now that we must guard against too easy a resort to a 'slippery slope' negative judgment. It is common for humans to want clear-cut ethical rules to follow, so that we know without ambiguity what we ought to do. Many Christians share this wish. It makes them prone to use the 'slippery slope' argument, and to say that any deviation from a rule opens the way for the abandonment of restraint and a slide into inhuman practices. But such certainties are rare in ethics, which allows for no more certainty than the complex nature of the issues permits. The ability to make careful moral distinctions is an essential part of what it means as a human being to grow to moral maturity; and therefore to Christian maturity. This is not to deny that there is *some* cogency in 'slippery slope' arguments, for widespread ethical attitudes usually have something to be said for them; but such arguments must not be given too much weight, and so become a stop to discerning decision making.

Beyond the area of more personal decisions lie the uncertainties and ambiguities of social, economic and political issues. Here there is a need both for professional codes of practice and public regulations; both subject to change with changing circumstances and further moral reflection. Public regulation is less flexible because more cumbersome to administer, often involving wearisome legal processes. Professional regulations are better because more flexible, except for very basic issues.

Failure to think about what should be done as against what can be done led the 'western' states in the economic boom from about the 1950s to the oil price shock in the early 1970s, vastly to increase the standard of living but to blunder about in the natural world in a thoughtless way. This has led to serious environmental and ecological issues, and to a rapidly growing public awareness, fuelled by a flood of books and reports. This was registered by the UN Conference on Environment and Development, the Earth Summit, in Rio de Janeiro in 1992. Problems are local, regional, and global. Locally, they include the securing of clean water, the safe disposal of waste, and the reduction of air pollution. These overlap with regional ones, which also include oil spills, acid rain carried by winds, and the contamination of rivers.

Globally, there is the building up of carbon dioxide in the atmosphere, with its effect on the temperature of the earth,

de-forestation and soil erosion, and the depletion of the ozone
layer by the human use of chlorofluorocarbons (CFCs). This last
was discovered over Antarctica only in 1985. Its effect is to
increase human exposure to ultra violet rays, leading to skin can-
cers and cataracts. In this case governments acted quickly. The
Montreal Protocol of 1987 provided for the cutting of the use of
CFCs by 50% by the year 2000, and now their use is to be phased
out by then. Those hugely populated countries, India and China,
could frustrate this unless the 'west' helps them to discard the use
of CFCs.

In the case of 'greenhouse gases' present levels of emission will
probably lead to a rise of $1°$ in global temperature by the year
2025, with a consequent rise in sea level. To stabilize the
concentration of long-lived gases will require a 60% reduction in
human use, which is very unlikely. The European Union would
like to stabilize its emission of carbon dioxide by the year 2000,
but not to reduce it. So the temperature is likely to rise. There will
be gainers as well as losers, and plenty of warning to both. The
process is slow. So is policy formation and its effects. It takes
about thirty years between decisions by governments to implement
a policy in this area and its results. The wealthy countries need to
make prices 'tell the truth', which a free market will not do, so
that the polluter pays. Equally important is financial and technical
assistance to developing countries.

Another problem is that of biological diversity among animals
and plants. The need for long-term goals has to be matched with
the lack of certainty in the evidence, and therefore of forecasts
based on it. However, one thing that can be wisely done is to
increase the area of protection for plants and animals; at present
this area is about 5% of the land area of the planet.

All these are serious issues but not apocalyptic ones. The
Club of Rome which has produced apocalyptic reports in the past,
has done it again in its *The First Global Revolution* (1991).[17] It
concentrates on the worst aspects of the present; the increased
gap between the richest and poorest states, the increasing number
of the poor because of population growth and the resulting
environmental destruction, and the corruption of governments.
Yet there is also an increase in life expectancy, adult literacy, and
in nutritional levels, together with a reduction in child mortality.

But these improvements are unevenly spread, and to mention them is no reason for complacency. Remember sub-Saharan Africa.

The UN Earth Summit did not achieve an Earth Charter, though the UN may do so in 1995, when it is fifty years old. But it did establish Agenda 21 as an action programme.[18] Responsibility must lie with the wealthy states which have the greater economic and political power; but not solely with them. And this brings us back again to questions of Trade and Aid.

Too many aid projects have been capital intensive, which suits engineering firms in donor countries and city élites in recipient ones. To raise this last point leads to being charged with paternalism, bred by the era of colonialism. The risk must be run. The World Bank has become much 'greener' since 1989. It has expanded its environmental staff, and now produces an annual environmental report, and has an annual conference on sustainable development. It demands National Environmental Action Plans, and refers to 'Global Environmental Facility'; all this is subject to the charge of paternalism. It cannot in any case satisfy the more radical 'green' movements, which do not want any disturbance of traditional established societies. However, the World Bank talks of 'capacity building', or developing managerial structures, which Third World countries often lack. Its Structural Adjustment loans, in response to the debt crisis since the late 1980s, have been concerned with the underpricing of natural resources and subsidies to energy consumption. But donors and recipients have different environmental priorities. The recipients want projects that will immediately improve the lives of their citizens, the donors are worried about global warming and the loss of diversity of species. They are too worried; the needs of the Third World are more serious. It is not surprising that this hinders the implementation of the 'Treaties' devised by the Rio de Janeiro summit on climate change and biological diversity.

Meanwhile the Non-Governmental Organizations have their own environmental impact assessment procedures. The World Conservation Union and the World Wide Fund for Nature in 1991 set out (with the Rio summit in mind) a document 'Caring for the Earth: Nine Principles for a Stable Society', together with a draft ethic concerned with the conservation of ecological processes of diversity. It refers to the community of life; that every life-form warrants respect independently of its worth to humans; that human development should not threaten the survival of other species or the integrity of nature, and to the relation of human rights to the rights of the rest of nature. The references here to stability of society and to the integrity and rights of nature brings us to an attitude to nature which regards it as an ecological homeostatic system, 'interference' with which by humans threatens disaster; and this leads to demands for a stable and not a dynamic society. And talk of the rights of non-human nature is related to this by a tendency to subsume humans into the rest of nature, requiring them not to 'interfere' with it. This attitude now has a lot of publicity in the 'west', and it has had a great deal of influence on the WCC.

An extreme example of nature considered as a holistic inter-connected system in which humans do not stand out is James Lovelock's *Gaia Hypothesis*.[19] (Gaia is either Mother Earth, or mother or grandmother of Zeus.) The earth is seen as a living being, the biosphere as a single unit in which environmental conditions are kept constant, from microbes to human kind. It is an automatic, unconscious, homeostatic, blind providence, with no reference to particular species, including humans. In short it is a scientific myth. There is every reason why it should be evaluated in the light of religious mythologies, but no reason why Christian theology should be awed by it as if it were a scientifically based 'fact' which has to be accepted.

A stress on the human is sometimes called 'speciesism' on the part of arrogant human beings. In particular they are charged with the oppression of animals. This has often been the case. Animals obviously have interests, which humans should respect, but that does not mean that they must be accepted without qualification. And have they rights?

Non-human animate nature is comparatively malleable, and far more than human nature can be governed or administered by humans, subject to the limits of prudence. Those who accept this in principle may well differ on how far prudence extends in responding to evidence. How well has the evidence been secured and on what criteria? On what criteria is it to be assessed? Is it prudent to take the worst possible case analysis? (This is what the military mind tends to do, and it is a main cause of the build up of armaments.) The ethical realm is peculiarly characteristic of human kind. What should be expected, indeed required, of it cannot be expected or required of animals, still less inanimate nature. This does not exclude respect for nature by humans, or imply that they may not have duties to it. What are the parameters of this? For instance, the fact that many non-human species have a nervous system and can suffer is itself a reason for humans to consider very carefully what suffering they can morally cause them. What are the parameters of this respect for nature?

Life is in many ways a continuum. There is not a total difference between humans and other species. Humans are prone to adopt some non-humans, in varying degrees, into the human fold, domestic pets for instance. But it is a somewhat arbitrary proceeding, and at times sentimental. Moreover the fact that there is no total break between species does not mean that there are not crucial differences between humans and the rest, any more than the fact that the phenomenon of twilight does not obscure the difference between light and darkness, or the fact of bi-sexuality obscures that between heterosexual and homosexual.

The existence of a moral realm is fundamental to human life. The Christian doctrine of conscience, which is a doctrine concerning all human beings, not merely Christians, is central to our understanding of the human species as persons. A distinctive characteristic of this is that persons are able to make judgments between good and evil, right and wrong, and know that they should follow what they judge to be good and right, and shun what they judge to be bad and wrong; and that when they fail to do this they are 'in the wrong', not because some external authority says so, but by a criterion they themselves acknowledge. This is to say that these judgments on conduct, though they are often faulty, are not just a matter of personal taste, but a response to a moral order which is simply a fact of human life. All attempts to explain it away, and there are some sophisticated ones, fail. Anyone who tries to act as if it were not so, quickly finds that in practice it is impossible to live consistently on such as assumption. None of this applies to animals, plants and inanimate nature. Their welfare overlaps with that of humans in varying degrees, and gives rise to some duties with respect to them. They can also threaten humans, and threaten one another in a competitive struggle within non-human nature itself. The idea that humans should not 'interfere' with nature is fanciful. Humans must respectfully order nature, under God, to promote human flourishing. In this sense it is proper to be anthropocentric. Cockroaches and disease-carrying bacteria are enemies of humans to be resisted.[20]

This is perhaps the place to refer to the feminist challenge to what in human history has been a dominant attitude; the men who are accused of oppressing nature are also accused of oppressing women, as much in the churches as in secular society. Women usually occupy the space left to them by men. Hence the rise of the feminist movement and of feminist theology. Hence the suspicion by women of many aspects of dynamic, technological cultures. New forms of reproductive technology are seen as a form of patriarchy, though it is doubtful that they are specifically so; rather they exist in the general context of a male dominated culture.

There seem to be broadly three forms of feminism. A liberal form concentrates on claiming political and legal status within the present order. A cultural one stresses the complementarity of men and women. (Some advocates of the priesting of women use one, and some the other, among other considerations.) Radical feminism sees the reproductive differences between the sexes as no more than a technical difference, and says that nothing less than a dramatic change in economic and political power structure is needed to reverse man-woman domination.

Feminism has always been a concern of the WCC, but it has had a much greater influence since about 1970. The WCC held a Consultation in Berlin in 1974 on 'Sexism in the 1970s', which led to it becoming a major concern of the Nairobi Assembly in 1975. This proposed a theological study on 'The Community of Men and Women in the Church', which culminated in a major Consultation at Sheffield in 1981 on that theme. Out of this a report came to the Vancouver Assembly. There are, indeed, some broadly similar ways in which oppressors oppress the oppressed, but to conflate their causes, linking racism, classism and sexism together, as was done in the WCC study is a different matter. It put them within the ambience of Liberation Theology (though it was some time before the Latin American Liberation theologians became alert to sexism). A major speech at Sheffield by the Roman Catholic Asian liberation theologian, Tissa Balasuriya, made the point forcefully. 'The struggle for change is *one* struggle. Racism, sexism and classism and all other forms of domination, rejection and marginalization are linked together in a demonic symphony of oppression'.[21]

It is very doubtful if this linkage was wise. As I have just mentioned, the oppression of women by men has been linked with the oppression of nature by men; presumably that of homosexuals by heterosexuals could be added if *all* forms of domination are linked in one symphony of oppression. In any case allying feminism with this all-embracing Marxist-type view of history has not been wise. It has left the ecumenical women's movement in the same kind of uncertainty following upon the collapse of the Soviet system as that of all those who had put their hopes in a better form of society which they thought had been hidden in it by Stalinist distortions. A simplistic feminist theology can obscure the assaults that have to be made against different types of oppression by race, sex or class, and in particular the specific challenges to embedded church structures and thought. Now that the feminist movement has articulated them they must be challenged from within by the resources of the Christian faith itself, just as the anti-slavery movement in the last century made the church aware of the implications of its own theological tradition which it had not realized. It was an example of the world setting the agenda.

Feminism stresses music, art, poetry, story-telling and socio-biography as embodying truth, and this can indeed correct an imbalance. But fancy can also creep in, as when we are referred to a supposed pre-patriarchal society about 10,000 years BC run by women. But allowing for the correction of an imbalance in Christian theology, which has come overwhelmingly from males and male-dominated societies, I have yet to find any insight in feminist theology which is altogether new in the Christian tradition, though women have not been in the foreground, and need to be. Also there is latent in it, a danger which needs guarding against. It seems frightened of what we may call 'universal reason', as involving an ideological exploitation of women by men. Here it joins a recent theological fashion for attacking reason in the status given it by the Enlightenment. That status may have been too simple, not sufficiently aware of psychological and sociological distortions. Yet the status of reason in humans, not possessed by any other species, is basic to our commonality, and fundamental to both our Greek and Judaeo-Christian roots in the 'west', together with the possibility of communicating with those of other faiths and philosophies. Although distorted by ideological considerations, from which it is rarely totally free, and therefore not as 'pure' as it sometimes claims to be, neither feminism nor any other trend of thought must be allowed to deny reason without challenge.[22]

What is the conclusion of reflections on these three areas for ethics? Briefly (1) a human ethic, including other species and ecological factors in its range, needs to be one of community and solidarity, and not the individualistic one which has become attached to the market economy, but is not integral to it. (2) Human freedom is not freedom to do what you like or to impose yourself on others, but is freedom from 'improper' restraints which hinder the exercising of responsible choices which go with mature adults. (3) Social institutions need to encourage human co-operative tendencies and to discourage human disruptive ones; the freedom of the market requires a strong social framework, and there is a place for coercion in it. (4) A common morality needs to be fostered among humans of all faiths and philosophies.

Religion gives a deeper dimension to these ethical requirements, both as an inspiration and a challenge. Christians may well think their faith is the most adequate interpretation of human experience, but it also is faced with these common requirements. The theme of the WCC, Justice, Peace and the Integrity of Creation, picked up these requirements. In the course of the next chapter we shall consider how it did so, and how adequate it was.

7 Where We are Today
2: The Recent Slogan and its Predecessors

I do not use the word slogan in a derogatory sense. It often has such a sense, suggesting thinking in crude headlines, and forcing analyses into simplified structures which obscure the inherent complexities of social reality. This is an obvious danger to guard against. On the other hand slogans can mobilize a mass of material into a convenient and coherent shape, as the basis for a relevant strategy on social issues, provided that the criteria by which the material is collected and co-ordinated are well grounded. The term 'ideology' is sometimes used for this process; if so it is in a neutral sense, not that originally associated with the Marxist use of the term to signify a conscious or unconscious distortion of thought and expression by the interests of ruling classes. It can be argued that ideological elements, akin to this, enter into all thought, and that it is an illusion to imagine that they do not. In any case greater self-and-social awareness can limit this, and the processes which have led to the formulation of the slogans we are to review were all of this self-conscious kind.

The recent slogan, Justice, Peace and the Integrity of Creation, is being slightly modified by omitting 'the Integrity of', and turning the slogan into 'Theology of Life, Justice, Peace and Creation', but its essential range and connotation has not changed. The three slogans we shall look at in rather more detail in this chapter are in a sense official, since they have deliberately moulded conferences and consultations. Three others have not had this status, but they have had an influence, which is still there in the present, and which warrant a brief consideration.

1. *Three informal slogans*

   (a) *Doctrine Divides but Service Unites*

This came from the Stockholm Conference of 1925. In the early stages of the Ecumenical Movement, when there was a legacy of isolation, indifference and hostility between the churches, and in the aftermath of the 1914–18 war, this affirmed an important truth. Faced with human misery, due to unforeseen natural disasters or humanly contrived ones, Christians who are separated from one another by church divisions but who together undertake 'ambulance work', find that as people they are drawn together, and begin to understand their different spiritualities beyond and beneath the separateness which church structures force upon them. Service unites.

But when longer-term social issues and policies arise, so do differences between Christians, who are as much divided ethically as they are doctrinally. This is because of the inevitable complexities and ambiguities of the issues, to which several references have already been made, and how doctrine is held to bear on them. Hence Christians who agree on doctrine, for example of the Incarnation or the Trinity, may differ ethically on almost any issue; on sexual issues, vegetarianism and war, to take three diverse examples. Service can divide, and doctrine unite. These differences often cut across church divisions. Nor are they necessarily irreconcilable. The Ecumenical Movement is itself witness to that. Doctrine and service both divide and unite; and attention has always to be paid to both. It would not be necessary to stress this too much if there had not been some recent tendencies to suggest a return to the Stockholm slogan, since denominational structures have proved so immobile.

   (b) *Let the Church be the Church*

Arising out of the challenge of Facism, Nazism and Stalinism, this slogan of the Oxford conference of 1937 retains its force as a challenge to tyrannical governments. It is also directed to those whose dissatisfaction with church structures is so great that they come to regard the church as an actual hindrance to a witness to the gospel, and leave. A generation ago this happened to a leading

English Roman Catholic theologian, Charles Davis. But all churches are likely to be faced with conscientious objectors of this kind. By contrast the Ecumenical Movement has promoted a strong and hopeful, but not uncritical, theology of the church. The Oxford Conference slogan was a challenge to the church to have the intellectual confidence and spiritual stamina to out-think and out-live destructive ideologies, and to defend the dignity of the human person against all that undermines it. However, it could be interpreted as 'triumphalist', an attitude only too common in church history; but in context that was far from what was in mind. There are, indeed, elements of triumphalism around. Vatican II took pains to disavow it, but it has not banished it from the Roman Catholic Church. Nor, to take two more examples, are the Church of England and the Church of Scotland free from it, though it is diminishing. The WCC cannot be charged with it. Indeed it has bent over backwards to avoid it. It should also be noted that the slogan is a challenge to the church itself not to be swayed by the spirit of the age (the *Zeitgeist*), but to use its theological tools for an appraisal of current intellectual and ethical fashions, not necessarily to approve or disapprove but to sift; being ready both to challenge and face challenges. It is not a demand that the church *must* so distance itself from public attitudes as to become sectarian. We have continually to ask how far this is being achieved, notably in the case of the recent slogan. We have also to ask what conditions in the State are necessary for the church to be free to be the church. Something like the moral framework of a liberal society is needed. Christians who attack this are in danger of cutting off the bough on which they sit.

(c) Let the World Provide the Agenda

This slogan came to the fore in the 1960s, without becoming official. It can be thought of as the counterpart of 'Let the Church be the Church'. In fact they point to the same aim; alertness by the church to 'what is going on', and critical reflection on it. This slogan partly arose out of the debate on secularization, analysed as a positive process, against inappropriate forms of control and intellectual barriers created in particular by those churches which were heirs of a Christendom situation, and their tendency to sacralize a situation over which they were steadily losing control.

Secularization in this sense was sharply distinguished from secularism as a one-dimensional this-worldly ideology, which has lost any sense of transcendence and in doing so has diminished the stature of human beings. The issue has moved on since then. Transcendence faces the challenge of Post-modernism, and humans are being subsumed into sub-human nature, to name only two current tendencies.

However, we should realize that in practice the world does provide the agenda. Theology is often thought of as if it proceeds from its own internal impetus, unaffected by 'what is going on'. In fact changing circumstances throw up new questions with which theology has to deal, and create climates of opinion which influence its thinking. Theology is never a matter of pure, unconditional thought; intellectual, social, economic, political and cultural factors all affect it. St Anselm's doctrine of the atonement cannot be understood without a knowledge of the feudal system. Why did the issue of slavery come to the fore in the last century and the emancipation of women in this? Be ready for the world to provide the agenda, but let the church also cultivate theological tools to appraise changing enthusiasms. And let these tools be sufficiently critical, so that they are capable of more than reacting to what the world may be putting forward, and too easily endorsing it. This is a danger in current discussions of humanity's relation to nature. The possibility must be held on to that the church can draw attention to issues the world has not seen, or is disposed to neglect.

2. *The Responsible Society*

This slogan is associated with the Assemblies at Amsterdam and Evanston. Evanston omitted 'The', making it clear that there is not one blue print of such a society in mind. We recall from chapter 1 that in pre-Amsterdam preparations J. H. Oldham had suggested a 'free' or an 'open' society. In the end 'responsible' was chosen, and defined as a society 'where freedom is the freedom of men (*sic*) who acknowledge responsibility to justice and public order, and in which those who hold public authority or economic power are responsible for its exercise to God and the people whose welfare is affected by it'.

It is a criterion, not a blue print. In the context of 1948 it had substance and at the same time avoided being merely anti-communist when the 'Cold War' was dominating international affairs. It rejected the ideologies of both laisser-faire capitalism and communism. It said that private property is not the root of corruption, as Marxists alleged, and that ownership of it is not an unconditional right, as capitalist ideology said it was. Evanston added that the state is not co-existent with society, thus allowing for the need to which the Papal Encyclical of 1931, *Quadragesimo Anno* pointed, with its concept of subsidiarity.

This slogan has many merits. It is realistic, but not utopian. It provides a yardstick by which to measure the *status quo*. It is not dependent on Christian faith, though it derives from it, and can attract allies from adherents of other faiths and philosophies. It reminds Christians that their stress on love must not by-pass justice, though without spelling out detailed programmes of what justice requires (which depend on changing circumstances). And it holds the person and the community in creative tension.

However, in the 60s and 70s Third World representatives, who had had no part in formulating it and some westerners, found it defective. It emphasized order and structure too much for them. It implied a gradualist approach when they were concerned with radical change. It seemed to stress political rather than economic justice (though economic power is mentioned). The political ideas underlying it seemed to be those of 'western' liberal democracy, epitomized in Reinhold Niebuhr's famous aphorism, 'Man's capacity for justice makes democracy possible, but man's inclination to injustice makes democracy necessary'.[1] The Third World was more interested in theologies of Liberation and Revolution. The slogan did not seem to fit when there was a conflict between public order and justice.

Violent change was not in fact ruled out by the definition, but it was not specifically mentioned. Violence was discussed at Mindolo in 1964, and Zagorsk in 1968,[2] as we said in chapter 2, analysed revolution more closely as (*a*) dramatic changes in the locus of power which need not, but may be violent; (*b*) all fast, comprehensive, and mainly unplanned, change; (*c*) protests of minority groups in particular countries.

The definition was re-drafted by de Vries after the Uppsala

Assembly to make clear it included making new structures. It then read that a Responsible Society is one which embodies the 'freedom of men who acknowledge the need to create new structures, enabling them to carry responsibility for all men, economic, social, political, national and international; where public order is the embodiment of constructive institutional change; and those who hold political or managerial power are accountable through appropriate organs to the people (including nations and mankind)'.[3] This has become a cumbersome statement in the effort to bring out more fully what the slogan intended. It never caught on. In the 1970s the situation moved away from it, and a new slogan was adopted at the Nairobi Assembly. But there may well be mileage left in it.

3. *The Just, Participatory and Sustainable Society*

In this comprehensive slogan Justice is, of course, not a new concern. It was there from the early days of the Ecumenical Movement, and is a perennial concern of Christian and indeed human, thinking. Sustainable is a new element. It comes from a Church and Society Consultation on 'Science and Technology for Human Development' at Bucharest in 1974. This was two years after the first Club of Rome Report, 'The Limits to Growth', which undoubtedly influenced it. Thoughts of a stable population, finite resources, zero growth, man's continuity with nature all figure in it. The time perspective is not clear – twenty-five years?, a hundred years? Nor are the problems of futurology dealt with. These issues have already been mentioned, and will be again. I say no more about them here. Participation came in through a vigorous discussion of the participation of the poor in history, as a messianic movement towards the Kingdom of God, expressed especially in the 1970s in the WCC programme on Urban and Rural Mission. There is a danger here, which has become clearer since Nairobi, that the poor may be sacralized, scientific knowledge ignored, and a surrender made to populism. This danger is illustrated by the content of a consultation on Political ethics called by the CCPD in Cyprus in 1981, and especially by the central part played in it by the concept of The People.[4]

The Cyprus Consultation pointed out that there has not been

a problem in the participation of professional elites (it might have said in 'liberal' regimes which are in part the target of the attack). Then it goes too far when it says that analytical models coming from 'western' patterns of thought and action make truth accessible only to experts, and to a process of understanding, prediction and control which exclude 99% of The People. (Similar complaints are made about clerical control in many churches over the 99% who are not ordained.) No clear way has emerged on how to integrate professional expertise with the struggle of The People. In the Marxist tradition Gramsci struggled with this, and coined the term 'organic intellectual' for those who identified with, and shared the struggles of, The People, as distinct from traditional elites.[5]

Pressure must come from below. The wisdom of The People provides the one sure resource for creative ethical work. They are the bearers of the possibility of overcoming aggression in the name of justice and peace. The People must be empowered so that they become the shapers of their own destiny. The 'signs of the times' must be discerned from a People's orientated perspective. The People are to liberate themselves from all forms of bondage and oppression, and create a new community of justice, self-reliance, freedom, compassion and celebration. The messianic Kingdom of God is the ultimate destiny of The People; they will transform political power under the image of the cross. They must take charge of their own economic and social well-being, and bring about something beyond representative democracy, power politics, capitalism and socialism.

In this dream the influence of Marxist thought of the proletariat as the innocent class because it has no one below it to exploit, is clear, together with its vision of a coming ideal social order where there will be no collective power (though now with the cross brought in to give it a Christian stamp). But who are The People? There is no suggestion of the Leninist differentiation between the class-conscious proletariat which is the instrument for pushing an inevitable historical change towards the ideal harmonious society, and the *lumpen* proletariat, which is too ground down to take any initiative, and for whom the class-conscious proletariat has to act. In the Cyprus document The People appears to mean all those not at present in power, treated as a coherent and unified sociological and political entity. Participation means recovering the roots of The People's story and its sufferings, articulating it, and in doing so comprehending its disclosure power.

Fanciful as this is, it embodies two challenges. First, special steps need to be taken by churches (notably the broadly middle class churches of the 'west') to hear 'the voice of the voiceless' themselves, not as interpreted by others. Next, the Cyprus Report does note in passing that there may be aberrations in what The People say, but that churches are only in a position to criticize if they understand its oppression and its struggles; whereas in fact they want to play a critical role without sharing them. The distant attitude to the poor of many Christian congregations bears out this criticism.[6]

Vast areas of Participatory questions in economic, industrial, civic and political affairs were not dealt with in the years from Nairobi to Vancouver, when this was the slogan. Indeed what was in fact done seemed to be suspicious of any form of indirect decision making associated with the principles of representative democracy. Then, with the elucidation of the slogan far from completed; it was faded out in a way which was never explicit, and was superseded after Vancouver by a new slogan.

4. *Justice, Peace and the Integrity of Creation*

The new words in this slogan are 'the Integrity of Creation'. Justice and Peace have rightly always been a pre-occupation of the Ecumenical Movement, and I shall say no more about either at this point. Sustainability remains on the agenda, particularly in relation to economic growth and environmental issues, and Participatory is pre-supposed rather than further explored.

In the Vancouver Assembly report there is only a passing reference to the new phrase, and it is a puzzle how it came to be taken up so vigorously shortly afterwards. It looks as if the enthusiasm of a few, probably including influential staff members, carried the day, when there was no similar *ad hoc* group for any other theme. But this is surmise. As a case study it would be a good example to examine the actual working of decision making processes in the WCC within its formal constitutional structure.

However, the theme has clearly had a growing resonance in public discussion, at least in the 'west'. It has now appeared in Papal and in United Nations documents. For some time the Third World was suspicious of it, as a device by the wealthy to keep their material privileges by rousing alarm at the global consequences if they spread to the Third World. Now the Third World has come to see that there are global problems from which it cannot be insulated. (In the case of another global issue, its former hostility to the GATT procedures has much abated, as it has come to see that there are more benefits for it in international free trade than they had previously thought.) Our present concern is with how the WCC has handled this slogan, which has become a lynchpin of its work; indeed there are attempts to make it *the* lynchpin.

The starting point has been an attack on traditional Christian attitudes to nature as being exploitative. An article by the mediaeval historian, Lynn White, has been constantly quoted.[7] It is open to some criticism, but its broad charge is supported by a major study by Keith Thomas[8] which establishes that in the sixteenth and seventeenth centuries, at the dawn of modern science, no intrinsic value was given to nature in theology or popular preaching. The charge today is that the traditional Christian doctrine of stewardship is too weak to protect nature (yet the word 'dominion' at Genesis 1.26, on which it is based does have a strong stress on human authority under God), and that a fundamental reconstruction of Christian theology is called for, so that creation rather than redemption becomes its foundation. Other major changes, though not necessarily connected, are often associated with this, such as a rethinking of the entire basis of economics, and a 'bottom-up' rather than a 'top-down' approach to nature. The tendency is to subsume humanity into nature. Yet nature commits crimes which a civilized world rules out for humans.

Traditional Christian resources are ransacked for evidence to support this new perspective. The more Protestant (now with some Roman Catholic help) turn to the Bible, the more Catholic, particularly the Orthodox, to the Fathers of the early church. The phrase Integrity of Creation cannot be faulted on the ground that it is not a biblical one, for the church had to go outside the Bible for a key term in expressing the doctrine of the Trinity.[9]

It is said that we need to re-read the Bible from the prespective of birds, air, water, trees and mountains, the most wretched of the earth in our time. We must learn to think like a mountain, to change our centre from human beings to all living beings; and that this has become our responsibility in order to survive.[10] In this confusion no indication is given on how humans are to think like mountains. (Note that in this new prespective human survival is still a central concern.)

Aboriginal spirituality is stressed. It sees God as more revealed in creation than in history (in contrast to Liberation Theology), and thinks spatially rather than temporally. In my view more anthropological evidence is needed on whether aboriginals do in fact live in such harmony with nature. In any case nature is not a harmony in itself. It is competitive and dynamic, and an arena of struggle. A difficulty with the term Integrity is that it suggests, even if it does not require, a wholeness and harmony which is not the case. Moreover the idea that plants, animals, water, the earth and the climate are a harmonious whole easily leads to a belief that they are inhabited by spirits – the ancestors of those now alive – who are present now. The sun and moon and the power of generation are present and can be a source of ancestral wisdom, spirits with whom a right relationship needs to be established. The well-being of all, past, present and future is inseparably locked. Neither the person nor the human community stands out. In all this we are near to shamanism (which, indeed, is attracting attention).

There are a variety of attitudes to nature in the Bible, especially in the Old Testament, both its friendly and its hostile aspects to humankind. Its internal competitiveness (Ps. 104.24), and its hostility is due to the Fall. Apocalyptic literature looks to a new earth, or perhaps a total transformation of this one, which will be harmonious. A certain fondness for apocalyptic writings has developed recently among Christians who are not fundamentalists (it has always been their hunting ground), though they write as if its hopes for the present earth are to be taken literally. Perhaps it is a way of coping with what seems an unmanageable or incomprehensible complexity. Another approach, already mentioned, is to stress creation rather than history. The Mosaic Covenant is downplayed in comparison with that with Noah and all creation, to which there are indeed fragmentary references throughout the Bible, but nothing like the stress on the Mosaic Covenant. God's divinely-willed order has been upset by the Fall. After it God makes an eternal covenant with all creatures, yearly re-enacted in a New Year Kingly Enthronement ritual in Israel, which is echoed in the Enthronement psalms (e.g. Ps. 99). Humans now have the duty to embody it in more than a king, and collectively to maintain justice, mercy and peace between humans and animals.[11] However, in the Old Testament there are passages where animals are simply human property, notably in the sacrificial system; and some texts which promise peace to humans *from* wild animals, not *for* them (just as peace is offered to Israel after the Conquest of Canaan).

This positive stress on animals is very different from both traditional and recent stresses on the personal in Christian theology, as in Aquinas, or Maritain, or Macmurray, to quote three rather different examples;[12] or from modern philosophies of the person in the Kantian tradition. The Pastoral Constitution of Vatican II, *Gaudium et Spes*, says 'All things on earth should be referred to men as their centre and crown.' The later Papal social Encyclical, *Centesimus Annus*, has a 'dominion' theology in relating humans to nature, with one paragraph on the environment. In the renewal of Moral Theology since Vatican II there has been a move from nature to the dignity of the human person as the centre of moral attention.[13] Similarly in the secular world, the UNCED Rio de Janeiro Summit said, 'Human beings are the centre of concern for sustainable development.'

Clearly an unresolved debate continues. Pope John Paul II had new thoughts when he issued the first Papal document exclusively on environmental concerns, for the 1990 World Day of Peace, entitled 'Peace with God the Creator, Peace with all Creation'. It assumes (*a*) a fixed relation between humankind and the rest of creation (from which much that is doubtful is sometimes deduced); (*b*) a harmonious universe with its own internal, dynamic balance (a homeostatic view which is questionable); (*c*) an order in the universe which must be preserved and protected (which is hard to square with the dynamism of evolution).

Biblical evidence points more than one way, just as it does on many other matters on which it touches, the authority of the state for an example. Biblical material has to be quarried as building blocks out of which a doctrine of humankind, nature and God can be built, just as it has to be on the state. In the past such doctrines have all pre-supposed a relatively static world in nature and in human society. A doctrine for our time must be able to cope with the dynamism in both. How far has the WCC succeeded in this task?

So far it has heavily endorsed one secular 'western' approach to ecological and environmental issues which has produced a flood of literature in the last twenty years. It has sought to give it a biblical and theological sanction. One example is a useful summary of the Rio Summit[14] (already mentioned) which assumes that plant life cannot sustain the continued economic growth of the rich economies, notes that the Canberra Assembly called for a lifestyle in harmony with nature, and says that a general ecumenical consensus has emerged with regard to human responsibility to care for a life in harmony with nature. It castigates the human pretension to define the centre of value in the universe, and calls for an eco-centred theology which sees God's spirit in all creation, rooted in the relational life of the Trinity.[15]

The efforts of the WCC to elucidate the meaning of the phrase 'the Integrity of Creation' has not been impressive, biblically or doctrinally.[16] It has followed too easily an intellectual trend of many readers of 'quality' newspapers and journals in the 'west', and has not built enough on previous work as the world has presented this new item for the agenda. There is much still to be thought out about humans having, under God, a respect and care for nature (as the doctrine of stewardship implies); and about the need to seek a consensus on the matter with adherents of other faiths and philosophies. The issues are important. Lady Thatcher once said vividly, 'No generation has a freehold on this earth. All we have is a life tenancy with a full repairing lease.' The *hubris* of the 1950–73 period must be corrected.

8 Where We are Today
3: Contending Theologies

There is nothing to be alarmed about in contending theologies. The Christian faith is many-sided. It is simple in essence, but paradoxical and subtle to express. It has a rich intellectual history, thought out against diverse cultural backgrounds, and it lives today in a variety of situations. Even if the churches were more united there would be diverse theologies, as there are within the main confessional traditions, including even the theoretically more monolithic Roman Catholic one. Contending theologies are part of the richness of Christianity, but they need to be tested against one another. Some were, and are, basically inadequate. Of these some have died, but others persist. It is unlikely that any one theology will be wholly adequate. Part of the task of the Ecumenical Movement is to show that this is so, and that we need one another, and none must have a tacit monopoly.

Traditional confessional theologies continue with variety in each of them produced by ecumenical contacts and world-wide social and intellectual change. The traditional Lutheran doctrine of the Two Realms is a good example, and in a different context I would discuss it separately. It can be, and has been, misused to promote an uncritical support of state authority, but so in practice can, and have been, other confessional theologies.

It remains of great importance, yet does not seem to have played as great a part as it should in recent ecumenical social theology. However, in this chapter I am less concerned with confessional theologies as such, even in the case of orthodoxy and the Roman Catholic Church, than with theologies which cross confessional boundaries. Even much of the internal debates within the Roman Catholic Church raise issues common to moral philosophy which theology cannot ignore.

1. *Christian realism*

This is the main theological stance underlying the Oxford Conference of 1937. Today, is it a hangover from the past or is it still cogent? Because in ecumenical terms it has a long history and was there in the pre-1948 days, it can be treated fairly briefly. There were, in fact, many strands woven into it at Oxford, which was remarkable for the range of its theological ballast. I mention some: Martin Buber's personalism (his *I and Thou* was first published in German in 1923); Karl Barth's theology of the Word (which sharply differentiated Christian faith from any other, and made it the enemy of 'religion'): Emil Brunner with his theology of the Orders of Creation (Family, Work, Politics, Culture and – oddly – the Church): in these humans are to live in responsible obedience to the command of God, given on each occasion in its immediate context, and on this Barth and Bultmann substantially agreed. There was the thought of Anders Nygren, sharply distinguishing between *agape* and *eros*, two different senses of the single English word 'love': *agape* moving from God and bestowing value with humans responding by faith, and *eros*, human yearning towards the transcendent. Also there was Paul Tillich with his method of correlation between the ultimate concern of humans met by the disclosure of God in Jesus the Christ: together with his insistence of the inevitable gap between the human grasp of the unconditional and the ability to express it, which lay behind his 'Protestant Principle', a perpetual protest against a claim to have encapsulated the faith in words or institutional structures which are beyond question. On the catholic side there was Nicolai Berdyaev, from the Russian Orthodox community in exile in Paris, with his understanding of radical freedom within the setting of the rich Orthodox understanding of *sobornost* (somewhat inadequately rendered into English as community or togetherness); and Jacques Maritain with his Thomistic philosophy of person-in-community. And perhaps we should add William Temple, with his Anglican incarnational social theology, tempered in the 1930s by the menaces of totalitarianism and mass unemployment.

Such a catalogue, perhaps almost incomprehensibly truncated, may serve to recall the theological riches behind the Oxford Conference. They can be followed up through the *Dictionary of the Ecumenical Movement* and its bibliographies. Within its variety it is Christian Realism, particularly associated with Reinhold Niebuhr, which comes nearest to capturing the approach to social theology at Oxford. I deliberately left out his name until now. He was particularly concerned with the relation of love and justice. The love embodied in the life and teaching of Christ transcends any particular social expression of it, but is at the same time always immanently relevant. Love which is less than just is sentimental; but justice never exhausts the possibilities of love. The potency of the expression of love is in inverse relation to the area of the attempt to realize it. That is why in collective life justice is the best approximation of love. Even in a family of several children each is loved, but it is still necessary to be fair between them. Justice as fairness is a fundamental human concept. It is because of Original Sin (an unfortunate term for a basic human reality) and the 'Fall' that love transcends all partial realizations of it, because it is never totally overcome in human life; for sin is at its most subtle when it feeds not on vices but on virtues. This is hit off in Mark Twain's remark, 'He was a good man in the worst sense of the word'. Ignoring this is what makes utopian thought and policies dangerous.

On the other hand Original Righteousness is just as much a fact of human life as Original Sin. There are not fixed bounds to human achievements under God, and to the quest for social justice which love motivates. Nor, of course, are there guarantees that the achievements of one generation will be maintained by future ones. Nevertheless Christian Realism is not a gloomy outlook, but a hopeful one. It is not disposed to be satisfied with things as they are; the Christian gospel has a radical challenge accompanying its good news.[1]

It is important to think in this way of the relation of love to justice. Because there is little directly about justice in the New Testament, biblically-centred Protestants are tempted to think too simply that love can be directly embodied in the social affairs of humanity, or to fall back on the Old Testament for rules of justice which are simply equated with the divine loving kindness. On the Catholic side there has been some tendency to assume that Christians *must* be just and *may* be loving; love then becomes a work of supererogation, to use a traditional term. A more subtle relation between love and justice is needed, whereby the changing adumbrations of justice are suffused by the more radical dimension of love.

In public policy questions churches must appeal to broad human experience. So must most governments, unless they rule a monolithic society. In 'Christendom' these have practically vanished. Even Poland and the Irish Republic are not what they were. Islam has some but, in the longer term, they also will probably modify. This appeal to the basic experience of human beings is what the Natural Law doctrine (properly understood) is concerned with. Such experience is personal to each human being, but corporate in that persons are what they are through their communal relationships. So living in communities of faith is of great importance in fostering commitments to love-inspired justice, and they thus have a vital role in contributing to the secular communities in which believers live cheek by jowl with citizens who follow other faiths and philosophies.

Public policies require verifiable information. Acquiring and assessing this information is always subject to distortions because of personal and social interests, and to hazards in forecasting trends and the likely effects of detailed policies. So a tolerable resolution of social conflicts is the aim, aware that these temporary resolutions will disclose new issues. In the process 'reason' has to be allied to 'interest'. We must acknowledge that there are other interests than ours that have to be heard in the public forum. Failure to allow for this can build up pressures until forceful conflict results; this easily gets out of control; and those who embark on rapid revolutionary change cannot control it, get swept away, and the end result is not what was intended.

Because of these factors affecting information, church teaching in this area is usually best at a middle level, between general statements and detailed policies, suggesting a direction in which to move rather than specific directions. Christian realism draws from its faith a profound understanding of the mystery of human life, and especially of the subtleties of sin and the depth and extent of divine grace. That grace extends beyond those who are 'one body in Christ' (to quote St Paul), for it is experienced as 'common grace' as we live in the organized structures of human life. It mitigates the sharpness of human conflicts. In public issues it leads to an awareness of creative possibilities, but also to a realization of the partial and provisional nature of particular judgments. Our reasoning in public issues (as in personal ones) is not as pure as we like to think, but is subject to ideological distortions. Awareness of this tends to reduce the tendency to self-righteousness. That is why it is unwise to derive political decisions too directly from the Christian faith. Nearly always they involve subordinate and relative judgments about 'facts' and tendencies which cannot be unqualifiedly sanctified as 'Christian'. Other Christians, equally concerned with the bearing of their faith on the 'common good', may come to different decisions. I shall return to this in the next chapter.

An important realization, latent in Christian Realism but not spelled out as forcefully as it has been lately, is the need in the pursuit of justice for what is often called 'a preferential option for the poor'; that is to say seeing that they themselves are heard in the public forum, not merely through the mouths of others; and this without either patronizing or sacralizing them. 'Poor' in this context stands for all marginalized folk.

2. *Biblicism*

Uncertainty on how to use the Bible for ethical decisions is endemic in Christian theology. It was most noteworthy in Protestantism, but now that Roman Catholic theology has become much more biblically conscious since Vatican II, it is evident there too. The Puritan revolution in England during the Commonwealth period is a good example of the Pandora's box which opened when the Reformers put the Bible into English and made it available to everyone. The teaching of the Bible dominated debates. Scriptural authority was expected for everything. In the year after the execution of King Charles I (strictly a judicial murder), a large number of sermons were preached on the basis of Psalm 149,[8] which speaks of binding their kings in chains. The New Testament was a prolific source of texts, especially Revelation which generated expectations of the fall of Antichrist and the rule of the Saints. Nor did biblical authority prove a problem. As John Hales said at the time, 'It is no hard thing for a man that hath wit and is strongly possessed of an opinion, and resolute to maintain it, to find some place of scripture which by good handling will be moved to cast a favourable countenance upon it.'[12] The result was a discrediting of scripture, and in the end the decay of a theological critique of the nascent commercial, and later industrial, capitalist society.

The WCC cannot expect to escape from this confusion, but it could do more to face it and elucidate it. It held a consultation 'From the Bible to the Modern World' at Oxford in 1949, and Faith and Order returned to the theme at Bristol in 1967 and Louvain in 1971, but nothing is explicitly brought from these to WCC studies in social theology and ethics.

The heart of the matter is whether it is acknowledged that it is not possible to move from biblical texts (or doctrinal affirmations for that matter), to a detailed conclusion on an ethical issue today without some intermediate step which depends on empirical evidence not obtainable from the Bible (or doctrine). Such evidence is *in principle* contestable, both as to its accuracy and adequacy, and the evaluation and interpretation placed on it, even though in practice this may not on occasion be seriously contested. Nevertheless, inherent uncertainties in the procedure make certain detailed ethical conclusions not possible, yet this is what churches and Christians often crave for, and quail at the thought of living by faith and not by sight. This accounts for their wayward use of the Bible. Even with such a clear command as 'Thou shalt do no murder' we have to decide what sort of killings are to count as murder and in what circumstances.

In the biblical drama of Creation – Fall – Redemption – Church – Last Things there are many different types of literature: narrative, myth, prophecy, apocalyptic, parable, allegory and proverb. Partly as with parables, the concern is with a radical truth told 'slant' to prompt the hearer to think in a new way. Partly, as with the Wisdom literature, the concern is with God's preservative activity, through a basic moral order, or Torah, less radical than *agape*, universal in the human situation and recognized to a greater or lesser extent in cultures which have no Judaeo-Christian roots, as is the case with China and Japan. Embedded in this literature are specific moral rules and demands, which are related to ther context and not to be taken as if they were timeless.

From the biblical drama we can properly derive belief in the fundamental dignity of the human person, and we can go further and see broadly how in the light of it humans should be treated and should treat each other. The slogan of the French Revolution – Liberty, Equality, Fraternity – is one succinct summary. But deciding how to express and balance these in particular situations requires empirical data. If we go further still and talk, for example, of the principle of 'the sanctity of life', the problem of balancing the claims of life against life, when they conflict, has to be faced. It cannot be 'applied' by deduction; evidence is needed. Talk of 'applying Christian principles' is common, and seems obvious, but it has to be analysed with care. In doctrine, applying Natural Law teaching meets the same problem. A traditional way, now much challenged, has deduced from the structure of the human body that the genital organs are intended for procreation (so that sexual intercourse must always be open to it); and that the speech organs were made for human communication, so that the tongue must not be used to lie. Very convoluted reasonings have ensued in trying to tease out these deductions in specific cases.

To return to the Bible. Of course there are a great number of ethical issues in the modern world to which it does not refer. Some of them are new; but in the case of a perennial one, like abortion, no clear text can be found. Of those to which it does refer, slavery and homosexuality are good examples. In the anti-slavery campaign in the last century there was a strong pro-slavery defence mounted on biblical grounds. It was allowed that slaves had to be treated humanely, but they are still private property and nowhere in either Testament is slavery explicitly condemned. Indeed it is actually commended in advance by Yahweh (at Gen. 9.24–27). The latest book known to me to take this line is John Murray's *Principles of Conduct*,[3] but he fudges it by saying the owner owned only the bodily labour of the slave.

In spite of the Bible slavery is now a dead issue among Christians. But Biblicists today use its texts in the same way to attack homosexuality as their predecessors used them to defend slavery. Leaving aside disputes about the exact meaning of some of the words used, and about what exactly happened at Sodom, and that Jesus was silent on the matter, there is no doubt that the Bible condemns homosexuality. But why does this settle this matter when it did not settle the slavery issue?

Let us take another example, the so-called 'communism' of the Jerusalem church, mentioned in Acts 2.44f. and 4.32. This is hardly ever quoted by Biblicists; it is too drastic. Those with property sold it and contributed to the common purse in which everyone shared. This appears to have been because of a vivid expectation, characteristic of the first Christians, of the imminent return of Christ, in a glory so lacking in his earthly ministry. The result was that the church impoverished itself by living on capital to such an extent that St Paul expended much energy in raising a collection among his Gentile churches for the poor saints of the mother church in Jerusalem (the deliverance of which was to be the occasion of his arrest). It is a classic case of a contextual policy, in this case based on a miscalculation and misinterpretation. But if this is accepted as 'time bound', as in the teaching on slavery, why not that on homosexuality? Even the Jerusalem church depended on an economy in which capital possessions could be sold; this is assumed, and any ethical problems raised by its institutions are not discussed. Or take Leviticus 25 and the Year of Jubilee. Much has been made of this lately, and it might have been the theme of the next WCC Assembly in 1998. The main provisions are: (1) Every fiftieth year everyone is to return to his holding. (2) The price of land depends on the number of years from Jubilee (like gilt edged stock). (3) This does not apply to towns; one year after the sale of a house in a walled town it is owned for ever. (4) This does not apply to priests; they have a perpetual right to homes in towns and in the common land surrounding them. (5) No interest is to be charged to a fellow Israelite. (6) Slaves can be bought from surrounding nations and their children can be bequeathed. (7) A poor fellow Israelite is to be treated as a hired servant and not as a slave, and is to return to his property at Jubilee. (8) A poor Israelite who sells himself to a rich alien or resident stranger is to have the status of a labourer on a yearly contract, and be released at Jubilee.

This is clearly an attempt to translate the ethical teaching of the pre-exilic prophets into a social order after the exile. Apart from the fact that there is no evidence of it ever having been implemented, it is unsatisfactory in detail (especially the differentiation between Israelites and others), and in one overall feature; it presupposes a static economy, returning to base every fifty years. Some will say, however, that it is the *principle* of Jubilee which matters. But what is the principle? Is it that the earth is the Lord's and not the personal fief of humans? Psalm 24.1 says that, and the whole Bible presupposes it. Moreover the teachings which Jubilee is trying to embody are those of the great writing prophets who were concerned to show that Israel could not presume on her special status with Yahweh to avoid the basic moral demands he makes on all peoples, and on the basis of which Amos condemns the surrounding Kingdoms (1–2.3). Jubilee is no special help here. Added to the fact that such a static concept is now inappropriate to modern dynamic societies, choosing to stress it is likely to lead to a strengthening of Biblicism, and a great deal of insubstantial rhetoric.

Dangers also arise in the attempt to produce an eco-Bible, fitting in with current environmental and ecological preoccupations. In fact the Bible witnesses to both the continuity and hostility between humans and nature, and within nature itself. The human 'domination' over nature (which has the strong sense of 'subdue') fits the struggle against weeds, to take one example. In the same way it covers both the violence and the self sacrifice in human life. There are a thousand verses in the Old Testament where Yahweh is depicted as engaging in acts of violence or force, and commanding others to be violent; but there are also the Servant Songs of Second Isaiah and, above all Jesus, who warns his disciples not to follow the rulers of the Gentiles who lord it over their subjects, and who himself came not be served but to serve (Mark 10. 42–45).

Also central to the Biblicist issue is the extraordinary variety of use made in Christian history of the concept of the Kingdom of God, central in the life and teaching of Jesus in the synoptic gospels. Part of the importance of this is that whereas the Old Testament reflects a one Kingdom situation, where church and state are one, the New Testament shows how Christians live in two Kingdoms, so that the relation of the Kingdom of God to secular Kingdoms is crucial. The *Dictionary of the Ecumenical Movement* lists sixty-three entries under Kingdom of God.[4] Here are some of the connotations to be found:

1. The church is the Kingdom.
2. The souls in whose heart Christ reigns is the Kingdom.

3. The co-operative commonwealth we are to build is the Kingdom.
4. The inspired guidance of the moment is a realization of the Kingdom.
5. The new future (*avenir*) of our eschatological certainty is the Kingdom, as distinct from any forecastable secular future (*futurum*)
6. The active commitment to the poor alone enables us to understand the Kingdom.
7. Suffering under the way of the cross is the ethic of the Kingdom.
8. A radical understanding of *agape*, always seeking expression and never fully embodied, shews the Kingdom as a perpetual radical challenge.

Meanwhile from the deconstructionist movement in literary criticism, which is allied with some philosophical and sociological tendencies called Post-modernism, comes a serious challenge to the possibility of any authoritative texts. I mention only the work of Jacques Derrida. He agrees that in practice we must bring some general grasp of an author's purpose in order to read any text whatever, but there is no guarantee that this understanding must indeed have been that of the 'author'. We need to be emancipated from any hypothesis about authorial intention. A theory must get along 'without itself claiming I fully understand what the other says, writes, meant to say or write, or even that he intended to say or write in full what remains to be read, or above all that any adequation need obtain between what he consciously intended, what he did, and what I do when "reading".'5

Here a necessary contextualism and relativism (which Biblicists ignore) has been carried to an extreme which has to be resisted. It certainly warns us that to get within the outlook of an author (or a writing) so as to see things through his eyes is a more precarious undertaking than many historians have assumed, in a noble effort to do that. But the fact that putting texts in their context is hazardous is not a reason for giving up the attempt. On the other hand there is more fixity about humans than Post-modernists allow for, a truth which Natural Law teaching affirms, and which theology needs to defend. Some recent stresses on narrative theology being highly specific to particular communities have gone too far. But to pursue this theme further would take us too far afield.

This may be the best place to refer to a radical social evangelical theology which has had a good deal of influence within the WCC. I have said that the contending theologies we are discussing in this chapter are not in watertight compartments. This one relates both to Liberation Theology and Eschatological Realism, which we are about to consider, but its use of the Bible can place it here. One of the noteworthy changes in theological outlook since 1945 has been the growth of social awareness among evangelicals. A large evangelical Congress on Evangelism at Lausanne in 1974 registered this. Many evangelicals are not ecumenically minded, but many are, and these have been influential within the WCC. They seem to repeat in their social theology the approach traditionally used in personal theology, which was a product of pietist movements in the last two centuries rather than a direct legacy of the Reformers. In preaching for individual conversion the preacher paints a grim picture of the human person, sunk in sin and totally in the wrong with God. Total conversion is the only way out. Once converted, the new Christian will make the right ethical decisions under the guidance of the Holy Spirit. There is no need to work away at the evidence, or wrestle with the ambiguities of choice; indeed the effort to do so might well be an effort to be justified by works and not by faith alone. Socially-minded evangelicals tend to concentrate on the dreadful disorders in modern societies (of which there are plenty), and to take a worst case analysis. They demand a totally new social, economic and political order. There they stop. How this is to be achieved and maintained, and the kind of structures within which the endemic problems of collective life occur and have to be dealt with are left vague. Indeed these endemic problems are not considered in the simplistic analyses, which in turn lead to utopian hopes. Moreover, because Protestantism has tended to be very, or exclusively, Bible centred, in a contextless way, this radically social evangelicalism is apt to raid the Bible for texts and select them in an arbitrary fashion. (It are not alone, of course, in doing this.)

Although it is never made explicit, this outlook seems to have had a great deal of influence on WCC work in the last decade or two.

3. *Liberation theology*

The rapid and explosive advance of Liberation Theology since the mid 1960s is indicated by the fact that a fifty volume *Summa* of it is being published. It claims to be a new way of doing theology, the way of *orthopraxis* (a term from the Marxist tradition). This requires active commitment to the cause of the poor as a condition for understanding the gospel and not turning it into an oppressive ideology. Latin American liberation theologians point out that that is exactly how Marian theology or the portrayal of the suffering and bleeding Jesus on the cross have been used. The next question is, having embarked on orthopraxis how do we know what to do in our present situation? We cannot find out from the Bible or the Christian tradition. We need a 'science' to guide us through the modern world. That science is Marxism 'Bourgeois' science is no use because values are brought into it which reflect bourgeois class interests, but Marxist science reflects the values of the workers, the universal class. Hence the need for Participatory Action Research (PAR) to give content to *orthopraxis*.

The case for Marxism is assumed, not argued. In fact a selective choice is made from Marxist theory. One version of Marxism stresses capitalism's historical role in bringing about the abundance of production so that the hitherto constricting bands of scarcity are overcome, and the classless utopia becomes possible. Libera-tion theologians, however, adopt a variant Marxist view, the Dependency Theory.[6] This in brief says: (1) Poverty in the countries on the periphery of the global economy will increase. (2) Inequality under capitalism will become worse. (3) World inequalities will inevitably increase. Evidence does not support it. In the decades 1970–80 and 1980–90 average real wages in developing countries rose by 1.3% per annum and 2.8% per annum according to the UN Development Report for 1991. On (2) the evidence is mixed, because of a bewildering variety between countries; wage inequalities grew in those countries which had minerals for export, where wages were relatively high. With regard to (3) in so far as this is so, the main factors are population growth (2–3% per annum in the poorer countries), together with bad trading policies by the rich countries and an urban bias in those of the poor.

Behind this choice of a particular version of Marxism is the wish to be as free as possible from international trade in favour of local self-reliance. This is echoed in many WCC documents. But Liberation Theology does not fit too easily outside Latin America nor does Marxist 'science' fit even there. Those oppressed by the *status quo* have not as much in common as the concept of The People as a unified one implies; blacks and feminists for instance. Different areas must find their own way to a preferential option for the poor, as Gutierrez (whose first book remains a classic on Liberation Theology) now agrees.[7]

The Vatican has issued two critiques of Liberation Theology through the Sacred Congregation for the Defence of the Faith.[8] It makes the obvious point that 'revelation' is the standard for Christian faith, not what in history helps the poor, but it does not meet the point that *how* to understand revelation and prevent it becoming an oppressive ideology is the issue. It stresses the location of sin as personal, but John Paul II has himself gone further than this in *Sollicitudo Rei Socialis* with a reference to structural sin. It says that the Exodus saga is not just about human liberation, that secular liberation can be oppressive, that eternal salvation is primary (as if that minimizes a temporal concern), and objects to the use of bits of Marxism, without acknowledging concepts like class struggles in Marxist theory. All this chips away at bits of Liberation Theology without facing the pertinent questions it does raise on the doing of theology, and the extent to which church structures are not geared towards a preferential option for the poor.

Since the 1970s the WCC has been embroiled in theologies 'from below', which start from the oppressed and not from the non-church secular man or woman of the 'west'. It has not been exclusively so, because there was the weighty conference at the Massachusetts Institute of Technology in 1979 on 'Faith, Science and the Future', though there has been nothing of the kind since. Instead there has been a certain polarization of contextual theologies from below, whether from Africa, Asia or Latin America versus what is thought of as 'western' or 'northern' ideological universalism. From Asia has come Minjung Theology, that of The People. From Africa there was the *kairos* document in 1985,[9] which has both gospel and Marxist roots. Tillich interpreted *kairos* in terms of the crisis and opportunities presented by the coming of Christ. Moltmann has used it to maintain that in theology we must not be tied to the restrospective language of the past but act in the light of a concrete utopianism, which views the world from a latency yet to come. So the present can be seen as a *kairos*, which is a mysterious moment of social, economic and spiritual force which resists both materialistic analysis and pietistic explanation. It is not a theophany, and it is quite possible for people to be unaware of it. One is reminded of Lenin's theory of seizing the right moment to push the revolution on (rather than waiting for inevitable historical forces to bring it about). The *kairos* involves discernment. In the Gospels the moment when Jesus came to Galilee saying 'The time is fulfilled, and the Kingdom of God has come near; repent, and believe in the gospel' (Mark 1.15) was a *kairos*. In political terms in South Africa it was to discern whether the situation was such that the time for a strong push against apartheid had come. The *kairos* thinking is a way of stating a problem continually faced by reformers or revolutionaries, but gives no help in resolving what is essentially a matter of insight based on evidence.

4. *Orthodoxy and social trinitarianism*

Orthodox social theology draws upon the christological and Trinitarian formulations of the Nicene Creed, the Definition of Faith of the Council of Chalcedon (451), and the works of the early Fathers. But it suffers from the legacy of Caesaro-Papalism in the Byzantine Empire. This was justified on the basis that as there are two natures in Christ, divine and human, and they are united without separation or confusion in one *hypostasis* ('person'), so the empire and the priesthood are 'a happy concord which will bring forth all good things for mankind', (the Emperor Justinian, 527–563). State and church are one. (This was the theory of the Tudor Settlement of the Church of England in the sixteenth century, brilliantly defended by Richard Hooker in his *Laws of Ecclesiastical Polity*, but an anachronism from the start.) It is much too direct a move from doctrine to politics, illustrated today by Moltmann's claim that a monarchical Trinity (see below) leads to totalitarianism; he also says monotheism does the same.[10]

Such a harmony as Byzantium claimed is unrealizable in any-

thing short of a static and monolithic state. After the fall of
Byzantium in 1453, and the chequered history of the Orthodox
under Turkish rule, the church was led to take a more pietistic
view, and then from the nineteenth century to identify itself with
the cause of nationalism. Hence the role of, for example,
Archbishop Makarios in Cyprus. In Russia the Byzantine formula
was used by the Czars to control the church, and when the
Bolsheviks took over in 1917 its position was not changed to any
great extent by the fact of the rulers being atheist, though at first
many priests were killed and churches destroyed and its property
suffered. The social witness of the church was confined to
supporting the government. It concentrated on survival and it has
succeeded. In eastern Europe some Christians interpreted the
Communist takeover as God taking away the material privileges
of the church because of their misuse, so that where before it
might have tried to free itself from at least some of its bonds, now
it was compelled to live in a ghetto of silence, and accused those
who wanted to break it of politicizing the gospel.

The upshot of this history is a lack of Orthodox literature on
this-worldly issues, a vast contrast to both Catholicism and
Protestantism.[11] When such issues are raised the tendency is to
appeal to the Fathers, particularly St John Chrysostom, as if the
wisdom to be found there settles the matter. Dostoievsky's great
novels do not raise issues of civic virtue; indeed one feels he
regards them as humdrum compared with the radical depths
which he explores, and that civic virtues may indeed lead away
from them. Berdyaev, and possibly Solovyev, are exceptions.
When Berdyaev joined the Orthodox exiles in Paris in the 1920s
new horizons appeared in his writing, much helped by ecumenical
contacts. The Orthodox, therefore, are in a weak position to help
with the reconstruction of the post-Soviet social order, except to
preach personal virtues in a rather pietistic tone, and to be
dangerously in tune with virulent nationalisms. Only in the USA,
where the Orthodox are now reasonably numerous and self-
confident, are they producing systematic social theology in the
context of current issues.[12] They have potentially great riches to
contribute, and close relations within the Ecumenical Movement
should lead to mutual benefits, and to contributions from
Orthodoxy in this area which are only beginning.

The Orthodox were just represented at Stockholm, but after that were more on the Faith and Order side. At Oxford they met Christians from the west, and also one another. The Moscow Patriarchate discouraged Orthodox from attending Amsterdam on the grounds that the Ecumenical Movement had been diverted from its task of reunion into social and political issues to catch souls for Christ by non-Christian means, a temptation which Christ rejected in the wilderness. In fact forty Orthodox were present out of a total attendance of six hundred and fifty-nine. At the New Delhi Assembly Orthodox from Soviet Europe officially joined, with government approval, accompanied by interpreters who were often thought by others to be government agents. In public they tended to make speeches in this area of a pietistic kind, for the government record. They were strong supporters, and the main financial backers of the Prague Peace Conference, and of the Programme to Combat Racism. At Nairobi they were put on the spot when attacks were made on the situation in the USSR in the light of the Helsinki and Madrid Conferences on Human Rights. In 1976 Father Gleb Yakunin founded the Committee for the Defence of Believers' Rights, parallel to Professor Yuri Orlov's Helsinki Monitoring Group. In 1965 he had accused the WCC of inactivity during the religious persecution of 1958–59, and in 1973 he appealed in advance to the Nairobi Assembly. His personal appeal was ignored (at least in public), but the general issue was publicly debated. We discussed in chapter 4 the problems involved for the WCC by the situation in the USSR.

A stress on the Social Trinity has been characteristic of Orthodox theology. 'Three persons in one God' is the traditional formulation. It arose as an attempt to put into words the doctrine which is a justification for believers in one God, worshipping that God through Jesus Christ. There cannot be two or three Gods, so the formulation is meant to safeguard this by saying Father, Son and Holy Spirit are three 'persons' in one Godhead. But 'person' is not used in our modern sense, but more akin to the word 'role', though that is not satisfactory either, because a role can be adopted and abandoned and is not a fundamental characteristic. God is at least personal in our sense, but with a richness of personhood which always expresses itself in these three fundamental ways. Clearly we are at the limits of language,

forced to say something of the mystery of God because, as
St Augustine wrote, we cannot be silent on the matter.[13] The relation of the human and the divine is not univocal but analogical.
And we must not turn an analogy into a model. There is talk of
God as a fellowship of three personal consciousnesses (in our
sense of personal), sharing in love, and then a corporate social
model of a human social order is deduced from this as if some
new source of information had been revealed. St Augustine had
used a psychological analogy of remembering, knowing and willing, which is better. The Social Trinity has been popular with
many Anglican theologians in the last century, and is taught today
by Jürgen Moltmann and some other Protestant theologians.[14]
This is dangerous, especially in contacts with Jews and Muslims.
The threefold nature of God must be subsumed within the divine
unity without equivocation.

The Social Trinity is popular in current WCC documents. No
mention is made of the issues just discussed. Rather, in a praise-
worthy effort to bring the Orthodox contribution into the mainstream of its work in social theology and ethics, there is a frequent
and somewhat rhetorical social Trinitarian emphasis, as if more
can be deduced from it than is the case; a greater reserve would be
prudent.

5. *Eschatological realism*

This is a term which has come to the fore only recently, but which
throws a lot of light on otherwise puzzling features of many recent
WCC documents. Its articulation seems to have been due to the
felt need to give some theological ballast to the general line of the
material coming in Justice, Peace and Integrity of Creation documents. It was made explicit in a booklet, *The Political Economy
of the Holy Spirit*, which was distributed to all members of
Sections 1 and 2 at the Canberra Assembly.[15] Its stress is on
the future Kingdom of God, as distinct from its past inauguration
in the ministry of Jesus, or present experience of its working
through the church as an agent of it. There is the insistence, now
familiar to us, of the need to abandon decision making on
the basis of present evidence. That is to be eschatologically
unrealistic. Instead we must make them in the certainty of the new

things God will bring about in the future. That is to be eschatologically realistic. We must go beyond the closed horizons of
instrumental reason in the power of expectant hope. We have
a praxis which is liberated from calculating its effectiveness in
political or social terms, a praxis that may seem 'irrational' or
'imprudent' to instrumental reason. Its natural context (as in the
case of Jesus) is not the arena of power politics or the competitive
market, but rather the everyday life of the people. Truth proves
itself by changing the direction of the present into that of the
future. Some of the most important events in human history have
been started as dreams, hopes, fantasies, expressions of the
creative imagination (pp. 22f., 60f.).

It is easy to see how symbolic actions, like fasting or boycotts,
follow from this approach. They surely have a place (even in the
calculations of instrumental reason!), but they cannot be the basis
of everyday, lay action in home, work and civic life. The root flaw
in it is that we do not know *when* God will fulfil his gracious
purposes for humanity in creation, or *how*; to what extent it will
be with human co-operation or despite the lack of it. Nor do we
know whether the apocalyptic language about this earth or a new
one is to be taken literally (unlikely, in my opinion). Nor can we
be certain *in what way* the resurrection (which was an 'event'
beyond time and space whose reality was effective and witnessed
to in time and space through the testimony of the apostles), is a
herald of our destiny after death, beyond our categories of time
and space, as Christian faith teaches. Modern scientific cosmo-
logies produce their own mythologies.

Moreover, the need to be aware of the limits of our knowledge
and of our powers of forecasting, and the need to be alert to
new factors is one thing, but to abandon decision making on the
basis of inevitably imperfect knowledge of present facts and
trends, is quite another. As we cannot know how or when these
'realistic' utopian hopes will be divinely realized, it becomes a
matter of sheer intuition as to what will prod the present towards
this realization. This raises all the familiar problems of one
person's intuition as against that of another. If someone affirms
that they have an intuition no one else can deny or disprove that
they have, but if they can give no reason for it, because instrumental reason is ruled out, there is no basis for dialogue with

someone who has a different intuition. We are back at Joan of Arc's infallible voice. This is extraordinarily like Marxists we used to have to deal with, who convinced themselves that some particular tactic or strategy in the present would hasten the coming of the classless society which the dialectic of history was bringing about in any case, a utopia which was in no direction related to the data of the issue in question (as understood by 'instrumental reason'). The disastrous misjudgments (and the cruelties) to which this led Communist parties in different countries is notorious.[16]

It is serious that eschatological realism has dominated so much recent WCC work, and that the present General Secretary is associated with it. It is sad that the WCC becomes aligned with attacks made by some both from the Right and the Left on universal instrumental reason, in its role of weighing evidence and forming policy. It is said to be a notion fostered by elites, money elites and the knowledge elites of the educated, who impose their prejudices on humanity. Instead we should follow what The People think. Macro issues are given up. It is the local that exhibits the power of eschatological realism. The local is more efficient than wider institutions; and it is a potential base coming from below which witnesses to a power of the cross which rules out power.

In the lively debate going on about modernity, religion, and rationality in the public realm, theology must not let religion and reason be severed. Doubtless the Enlightenment had too simple a notion of abstract rationality; but mistrust of reason, even in favour of love, can open the way to hate, and provides no basis for justice. Reason must not be thought of narrowly as the power to make logical deductions from a particular premiss; it must include the power of discernment. Coleridge called this the imagination, and held it to be the agent of reason. This is an issue of fundamental importance. The attack on instrumental reason is misguided.

6. *Recent debates in moral theology in the Roman Catholic Church*

Something more needs to be said, beyond what was covered in chapter 3, on a large theme which ideally requires fuller treatment. On the *content* of Roman Catholic social theology we recall that the church has gradually taken on board 'western' democratic ideas of participatory society (though hardly in the church itself). A preferential option for the poor was taken up by the Synod of Bishops in 1971, and is expressed in the Encyclical *Laborem Exercens*. The Vatican Instructions on Liberation Theology underplayed the positive contribution of Marxism to an analysis of private property and social conflict, but the influence of that theology is shown in *Laborem Exercens* and *Sollicitudo Rei Socialis*. Also the bishops in the USA pioneered a more nuanced and detailed analysis of the economic order, and on nuclear warfare; they said their work was on the level of prudence, where Christian opinions may well differ. The New Right said they had been hijacked by the new administrative and social work class in the public sphere, with its interest in state run projects. Feminists deplored that affirmations about women were advanced without their participation, or the recognition of the social role of fatherhood; and that the use of Natural Law doctrine in Vatican teaching on sexual issues is patriarchal.

One of the preparatory papers for the Council was on the moral order, with a stress on precise precepts and prohibitions binding on all humans, known through Natural Law, especially as interpreted by official Papal and Vatican 'replies' to specific questions, and often reinforced by church law. These precepts are timeless, a-historical, regarding certain acts as intrinsically evil, irrespective of context. To deny this is to fall into the sheerest relativism. This document was thrown out when the Council met – together with all the other preparatory documents – and it is scarcely reflected in the Council's proceedings. But the issue came to a head again over the issue of conraception. In his encyclical, *Humanae Vitae*, Paul VI reiterated the prohibition of artificial contraception, calling it *intrinsece inhonestum* and never permissible, regardless of context or intention. This was contrary to the advice of the Papal Commission which had been created to take the issue out of the sphere of the Council. In its report to the Pope, that Commission had recommended that, other things being equal, artificial contraception could be considered admissible in the context of a marriage where the fundamental relational and procreational values of marriage were being fully respected. The rejection of this position by Paul VI was seen by many Roman Catholics as an unacceptable exercise of teaching authority. Although most of *Humanae Vitae* embraced the very person-centred approach to marriage which had been developed in the Council, the justification for the prohibition of artificial contraception seemed to revert to the kind of moral theology which had been rejected at the beginning of the Council. Consequently, the controversy that has raged since has not been about the issue of infallible church teaching. (It is interesting to note that Vatican II locates infallibility in belief in the whole People of God and recognizes that, under very strictly limited conditions, infallible teaching pronouncements can be made by the college of bishops, speaking together, or through the Pope speaking with his authority but in the name of the college of bishops.) The focus of the controversy has been the authority of non-infallible teaching on moral issues which do not concern the core of Christian faith, and when this teaching seems to be based on an approach to moral theology which is strongly debated among moral theologians, and many of them regard it as unacceptable. The situation is aggravated when the Vatican wishes its teaching statements to be treated with such respect that public dissent by theological moralists is almost ruled out. It is this attitude which makes relations with the WCC difficult in practice, as we saw in chapter 3.

The debate since Vatican II has been between revisionists, who interpret the call of the Council for a renewal of Moral Theology in a radical way, and traditionalists who want it restated more cogently. The Encyclical *Veritatis Splendor* (1993) is an attempt to do this, with hints of disciplinary action latent. The traditionalists, however, have raised an issue in the realm of Moral Philosophy which it is important to note, because Christian moral reasoning cannot afford to set itself apart from Moral Philosophy, as it is tempted to do (and much WCC work in this area does), for it is in the area of 'practical reasonableness', where Christians live alongside other human beings of varying faiths and philosophies. Sexual ethics has been the focus of much of the debate, but not all; indeed it covers all issues.

'Practical reasonableness' seems a sound and straightforward term, starting from which traditionalists argue that there are certain basic human goods, self-evident to human reason. We must never destroy or impede or damage any of them in any decision, or the result will be self-alienation instead of self-integration. These values can be embodied in exceptionless prohibitions. For example, never lie, even to prevent a murder; never try artificially to prevent conception in sexual intercourse. It is argued that it is impossible to weigh one basic value against another, for they are incommensurable. Hence trying to weigh a balance of the different values and disvalues to be considered in deciding what to do (often called proportionalism) is impossible and corrupting. The moral is, stand by the non-infallible teaching of the church.

It seems clear that the Encyclical *Veritatis Splendor* will not stop the argument. The traditionalists' case does not convince a large number of moral theologians. Internal power structures in the church are at stake. This internal pre-occupation does not bode well for ecumenical co-operation, for the Vatican is on one side of the debate and the side that makes co-operation difficult. It does not appear to be open to a genuine dialogue on the matter within its own church or with others.[17]

9 Questions of Method in Christian Social Ethics

If there are contending theologies there will be different approaches and emphases in ethics, whether personal or social (in so far as these can be conceptually separated). For example, some want to move deductively from the Bible or doctrine to issues in the modern world, others want to work inductively from contemporary data back to basic biblical and doctrinal affirmations. Both positions have their problems. In my judgment it does not matter where one starts so long as both elements, biblical-doctrinal and empirical data, are brought together so that in reflecting on both they reciprocally influence one another. Some ethical theologies are more concerned with building up a *koinonia* ethic within Christian congregations, others with the way in which Christians can contribute to a common human flourishing in plural societies and a plural world. Neither should be pursued exclusively. Some ethical theologies are almost wholly concerned with the radical prophetic witness of the church; others see it as a vital conserving influence, supporting basic social institutions against dangerously fragmentary tendencies in civil society. It must be both. But how can we discern what mix is appropriate in particular contexts? And how can we remain alert to the dangers of each approach? Some ethical theologies focus more on the decisions of lay folk in their families, jobs and civic roles; others focus on church resolutions and Christian pressure groups. Some emphasize the local and unofficial, others the more official and higher level activity. There is room for a variety of stresses. They are all aspects of 'the Church and its Function in Society', to quote the title of the preparatory book for the Oxford Conference of 1937, referred to in chapter 1. In this chapter I take up some problems under this heading which were not fully dealt with in previous chapters, and which will arise whatever differences of emphases there may be in theological social ethics.

1. *The primary reality of the church*

I begin by recalling what has already been said on the centrality of the church and its worship. As William Temple said, worship is primary and conduct tests it; always provided that it is not complacent worship, but worship which is both an inspiration and strength, and also a challenge and spur to action. That is why renewal as well as unity have always been the twin targets of the Ecumenical Movement. All the traditional elements of worship – adoration, thanksgiving, penitence, intercession and petition – are involved in the way we are built up together as Christians to be a community of persons of discernment in finding out and following what the Christian faith requires in daily living. A leading ecumenical theologian has said, 'We are more likely to worship our way together to a new reality than we are to think or resolve our way there.' That is true as far as it goes. We could create a new slogan 'Worship unites and decisions divide', so long as we remind ourselves that decisions must be made, and that we have to live with fellow Christians who differ on them. The worship at the Vancouver and Canberra Assemblies was a moving illustration of this. The WCC had done a fine job in enabling those present to share this reality. Just because Christians are likely to be divided over ethical decisions (for reasons already mentioned several times and which will be discussed further in this chapter), it is vital that they be held together in common worship through Jesus Christ. It should lead to ecumenical trust, and to a mutual strengthening and correction rather than suspicion. Since worship, like all human activities, is flawed it does not always achieve this, but nothing else is in as good a position to do so.

The problems connected with thinking about, and making decisions on, current issues arise, to summarize briefly, from four aspects of social life. (1) Acquiring the necessary data, which means arriving at criteria by which to select out of the myriad facts of social life with which we are surrounded, those which are relevant. (2) Deciding what varying weight to attach to those we do pick out. (3) Suggesting what general direction policies should go in the light of our analysis and of our estimates of the consequences of the possible lines of action open to us. (4) Carrying this process further into advocating detailed policies.

All this is subject to ambiguities, errors and distortions. The information needed (the 'facts') may not be sufficiently available or clear, and yet decisions cannot always wait; and it can be mis-interpreted, because our perspective is distorted by personal or corporate ideological considerations. The church as a sociological reality has her own corporate interests, spectacles through which she looks. Just as churches need to be open to dialogue with, and correction by, other churches, and from the criticisms of outsiders, so does each Christian. As far as churches go this is what the WCC has in mind when it talks of a 'conciliar process' (properly a pre-conciliar process); and when it talks of 'covenanting together' it should mean churches committing themselves to work and wit-ness in a particular area of human and Christian concern, racism for example, and for the most part to the advocacy of general policy directions. Detailed policies are a better field of operations for special interest groups within a church, between churches, or between churches and what we can broadly call secular groups, when churches co-operate with those of other faiths and philo-sophies.

Similarly lay folk can work at a more official church level, or in church action groups, or in secular ones, and above all with those in the structures within which they find themselves in civic life as fellow workers or managers and fellow citizens. Not everything has to be done under an explicitly Christian banner, nor do Christians have continually to be concerned that what they say is so distinctively Christian that no one else could have thought of it. Indeed it is of prime importance to identify allies, on the basis of some understanding of a common morality and its social implications, between Christians and those with whom they are bound together in civic life in the bundle of humanity. Christians have every reason to suppose that God wishes human life to flourish, and has put us in this world in the first place not as Christians but as human beings. So while Christians must want to share what they believe to be the good news of the gospel and not keep it to themselves, they have an equal need to discern what is needed to further the human flourishing which God intends for all persons made in his image (to quote Gen. 1.26). This does not exclude concern for nature, but that is not the focus of the present discussion, and in any case is best approached in the context of an understanding of the place of person in the divine economy.

2. Prophecy and doctrine: Their essentiality and their limits

In the previous chapter I considered the need of intermediate steps in moving from a biblical text to an ethical issue today. I referred to the different types of literature in the Bible. Here I say something about only two of them, prophecy and apocalyptic. They are clearly related. There is much stress today on the prophetic role of the church, notably in WCC literature, to the almost complete neglect of its conserving role in the Bible, as represented by, for example, the Wisdom literature in the Old Testament and the Pastoral Epistles (I and II Timothy and Titus) in the New Testament.

What is the meaning of biblical prophecy for today? Biblical prophets used words and symbolic actions. I am mainly concerned with words, but actions must not be forgotten. Examples of it include Jeremiah buying the ancestral field at Anathoth in a very public manner from his cousin, and telling his secretary Baruch to preserve the deed carefully as a sign of his confidence that there would be civilized life there once again after the disaster he saw coming (Jer. 32.6ff.); or Ezekiel shaving his head and his beard, dividing the hair into three parts, and burning one third publicly in Jerusalem (Ezek. 5.1ff.). There will always be a place for symbolic actions designed to call public attention to realities which it ignores. Efforts have been made in recent years to draw attention in countries of the 'west' to conditions of homelessness among their own citizens, or famine in Third World countries, or the state of refugees; one example is prophetic individuals or groups living in spartan conditions, such as tents, in prominent public sites.

As to words, the prophets addressed Israel as a church-state. They were concerned with the inescapable moral demands which Yahweh, of his very nature, must require of all human beings. In the case of Israel as a church-state, convinced of God's covenant election and of her special place in his purposes for humanity, there was the temptation to rely on this and avoid the ethical challenge. To combat this the prophets linked belief in

Yahweh to ethical obedience so firmly as never since to be
separated. There are left in the Old Testament, despite its various
recensions, examples of insufficiently ethical belief, and also of a
basic ethical insight which stands in criticism of religious belief,
notably Abraham's dialogue with Yahweh over his proposed
destruction of Sodom, good and bad alike (Gen. 18.20ff.) 'Shall
not the God of all the earth do *right*?' In so far as Israel was a
'chosen people' the prophets held that their ethical responsibility
was all the greater. But the ethical norm was a common morality
by which the prophets in the name of Yahweh judged other states,
although they accepted other gods. Amos 1–2.3 has already been
quoted.

The prophets were primarily denunciators. But they did
promise either the remission of disasters, which Yahweh had in
store for his ethically rebellious people, or comfort after disaster,
on condition of a complete transformation of conduct. They had
no detailed policy recommendations, or middle level proposals. In
foreign affairs Israel was to rely solely on Yahweh and not get
embroiled in international relations. In home affairs a complete
moral reformation was needed. 'Cease to do evil: learn to do
good.'

How could one discern the true from the false prophet in the
welter of prophecy? No workable test was ever found. One was
that a prophet who spoke of smooth things instead of disasters
was a false prophet. The other was whether what the prophet said
would occur did in fact happen. But that is no help in discerning
at the time.

When prophetic hopes of a thoroughly morally transformed
Israel failed, after the exile prophecy turned into apocalyptic.
Yahweh himself would have to act when humans had shown
themselves impotent. In the New Testament prophets in the early
church seem to have a similar outlook. They were adventists looking to the imminent return of Jesus in glory to exalt the righteous
and confound the wicked. When these hopes faded prophecy
faded and became absorbed into the general pastoral and teaching
role of the church.[1]

Biblical prophecy is not a direct model for the church today. It
has to be seen in context as an absolutely crucial stage in the
deepening of Israel's understanding of what belief in Yahweh

involved. Without it Israel's religion would have disappeared, like that of neighbouring states such as Moab or Ammon, and it would never have recovered from the disaster of the exile in Babylon. And as to adventism, which has been endemic in sections of the Christian church, we do not know how to interpret 'Christ will come again'; that is how or when God will fulfil his good purposes for creation. Today we need witnesses rather than prophets, witnesses to the radical challenge of the Kingdom of God brought near in the teaching and life of Jesus.

How does it stand with respect to apocalyptic? It flourished in the inter-testamentary period in Judaism, and was clearly an important element in the early church, as the eventual inclusion of Revelation in the New Testament witnesses. It looked not so much to the fulfilment of history as we experience it, but to its end.

The absolute future it is concerned with is discontinuous with the present. It claimed some knowledge of when divine intervention to wind it up would take place. So its view of present history was pessimistic; it is of little significance. Things will get worse before Yahweh intervenes. Believers at best can hang on, if they are not martyred. They can be certain of their place in the post-apocalyptic order, and it is mostly thought to be an exclusive place. There is satisfaction that those excluded get their deserts. It is not easy to transfer this outlook into the modern world in any direct way. If it is a way of affirming that God will indeed fulfil his good purposes disclosed by Jesus Christ, that is a central witness of the New Testament, and does not specially need apocalyptic.

The legacy of prophecy is a stress on radical transcendence of the gospel. It goes beyond the morality of the eighth-century prophets to the prophetic legacy in the teaching of Jesus. This includes common morality but takes it further so that it becomes uncommon and paradoxical. The strenuous commands of the Kingdom of God are in keeping with the radical understanding of God and his paradoxical rule in the world in which Jesus lived and taught. It remains as a seed sown in the world, a reality striving to be expressed in human personal and collective life, never completely realized, and always facing us with the challenge to take it further. This is of immense importance for churches, who find it difficult to be self-critical. It has taken the Roman Catholic Church nearly four hundred years to admit it was wrong in its treatment of Galileo. Orthodoxy has no tradition of a 'prophetic' ministry in the public forum. It understands philanthropy, that is to say 'ambulance work', which is indeed necessary, but is not sufficient. On the other hand moving too simply from biblical prophecy to the modern world can lead to denunciations of everything that is wrong in the world (a formidable list), followed by demands for a totally new social, economic and political order, accompanied by simplistic social, economic and political analyses. It is all too easy. It avoids the task of working to find the best policy options which are available in particular contexts.[2]

If we move from types of biblical literature to doctrine, all the classical divisions of Christian theology – Creation, Fall, Redemption, Church and Sacraments, the Last Things – arise from the fundamental disclosure of God's love (*agape*) in the person and work of Jesus Christ. Their bearing on human society has been interpreted in five ways in the course of Christian history, analysed in the classical study by Richard Niebuhr *Christ and Culture*.[3] All have cropped up so persistently that we must surely assume that they all have relevance in certain situations. But that does not mean that all are equally cogent. All are based on the same biblical data. All, except the Christ of Culture type, can be interpreted in conservative or radical ways, according to basic assumptions about the church (explicit or implicit), and a reading of the evidence concerning a particular cultural situation. In view of the radical challenge of the Kingdom of God a strongly conservative view of the *status quo* is hard to justify unless there seems no feasible alternative to it at a given time which would not be worse.

This raises the question of how far the church should be a conserving and how far a change agent? It is significant that a conserving stance has been so common. It is true that order is basic to human flourishing. In a state of anarchy no human projects can be completed. The weak are at the mercy of the strong, and the honest at that of the unscrupulous. Nevertheless, churches have been too fearful of disorder and too tied to continuity. This has become increasingly inappropriate at a time of rapid social change which has now been endemic for more than two hundred years in Britain, and has spread world wide. Established order can come to be seen by many as disorder, and unless means of orderly change are provided discontent leads to revolt against the order which was being protected. And revolutions, once started, easily get out of control and end not where their instigators intended.

How these classical Christian doctrines are interpreted is influenced by the cultural context in which they are received. As I have mentioned there is a reciprocal influence between the two. This circularity is inevitable. But without going into the matter more deeply than is feasible here, it is possible to see a continuity in the doctrinal tradition because of some basic continuities in human life. We can ask meaningfully on its basis such questions as, How should persons by treated by those in authority? How should they treat one another? Certain broad principles emerge which have to be filled out in detail in different contexts. William Temple did this in his *Christianity and Social Order* of 1942. The most recent solid attempt to do it has been in Papal documents. It started in *Octogesima Adveniens*[4] in a paragraph which is worth quoting:

> In face of such widely varying situations it is difficult for us to utter an unified message and to put forward a solution which has universal validity. Such is not our ambition, nor is it our mission. It is up to Christian communities to analyse with objectivity the situation which is proper to their own country, to shed on it the light of the Gospel's unalterable words and to draw principles of reflection, norms of judgment, and directions for action from the social teaching of the Church.

Paul VI goes on to say that it is up to these Christian (*sic* Roman Catholic) communities '. . . in dialogue with other Christian brethren and all men of goodwill to discern the options and commitments which are called for in order to bring about the social, political and economic changes seen in many lands to be urgently needed'.

John Paul II subsequently took up the same line of thinking, for example in *Sollicitudo Rei Socialis* (par. 41). It is acknowledged that the church is not a political or economic expert. The Roman Catholic bishops in the USA, thinking along the same lines, said that their ventures into these realms were at the level of prudence, where Christians might well disagree with one another. Both they and the Pope say that in these areas it is necessary to draw on the work of the social sciences, but they seem to assume that the evidence from the social sciences will agree with what the church teaches from its own premises. A more nuanced criticism of the social sciences is needed because sometimes there is imported into their work positivistic assumptions which do not derive from their discipline but from a secularist faith; on the other hand Christian theology is liable to overcall its hand and cramp the social sciences by imposing its framework on them.

I return to Paul VI's analysis in *Octogesima Adveniens* of three contributions which the church makes to the process of decision making; and their repetition in subsequent Papal documents.

(a) *Principles of reflection*

Values of truth, freedom, solidarity, justice, peace and love are referred to (similar to the way William Temple or Paul Ramsey proceed). All derive from the dignity of the person. So do human rights (and duties for that matter). But persons are what they are through a community of persons. So they are inter-dependent. An organic understanding of society is involved, according to which each is to contribute to the common good; it is to be a conscious contribution, not one achieved by an 'invisible hand' as each pursues exclusively his own interests. Public authorities are to foster the common good. This understanding is contrary to the individualist philosophy of the New Right. It is probable that the concept of subsidiarity, mentioned in the third chapter, comes in here, stressing human participation at every level in social decision making; so may the universal purpose of human goods, which limits the place of private property according to its social function (a point R. H. Tawney stressed forcefully). It is also possible that John Paul II's stress on the priority of work, in *Laborem Exercens*, belongs here together with the priority of labour and of an adequate wage level over capital and profits, though modified in later documents like *Centesimus Annus*. I am not certain what exactly does belong under this heading, but the general drift is clear on the 'principles' by which Christians are to reflect on the working of economic, social and political structures.

(b) *Norms (or criteria) of judgment*

I am not sure how these differ from principles of reflection. Perhaps the dignity of the person in community, and the values that need to be pursued to express these, alone belong to the principles of reflection and the rest to norms of judgment. I do not know. However, it is clear that there is no blueprint of a Christian social order in mind. Judgments have to be made on the basis of principles and norms and in the light of an analysis of particular situations. New situations require a fresh evaluation.

(c) Directions for action

It seems clear to me that these can come only from the thinking and practical experience of those involved, together with an element of necessary expertise. This raises all the problems of dealing with empirical evidence to which I have frequently referred.

All this needs clarification. It seems as if under 'criteria' and 'directives' the Popes are bringing out the necessity and basis of practical reasoning and of making careful dinstinctions in moving from doctrine to conclusions on current issues, and a middle level between generality and detailed recommendations. The church cannot play safe and remain at a purely general level; yet as soon as she goes further she runs into problems which cannot be avoided. Jacques Maritain expressed this well:

> The closer to concrete circumstances a moral agrument comes the more difficult it is to formulate a clear and certain conclusion. Moralists are unhappy people. When they insist on the immutability of moral principles they are reproached for imposing unliveable requirements on us. When they explain how these immutable principles are to be put into force they are reproached for making morality relative. In both cases, however, they are only upholding the claims of reason to direct life.[5]

Moral theology is involved in the same problems as moral philosophy in dealing with particular issues. It has to hold to some basic assumption about human beings. It can move from this base to the discernment of particular issues, or move from the data of the issues back to the basic assumption, clarifying both in a process of mutual refinement. The basic assumption will affect the selection and weighing of evidence. Christians have good reason to suppose that their assumption can in principle be shared by all who examine their own living experience of what it is to be a human being. Christians relate it to their understanding of God. Others will have a different basis; either a different doctrine of God which overlaps with the Christian one at this point, or a secular humanist one. There are attempts to deny any universal human understanding in this sense by those who carry a necessary emphasis on relative and conditioning factors too far. But this cannot be pursued further now.

It is by this kind of careful reasoning that 'slippery slope' arguments are dealt with. Proponents of it want to take a clear-cut stance, and are opposed to the careful distinguishing of cases by moral reasoning. Such reasoning attempts to be comprehensive in the range of issues covered, and consistent between one issue and another in the way they are tackled. For example we should not forget the way we think about persons in medical ethics when we consider the way we should think about non-human nature. It is also necessary to defend the status of human moral reasoning against those who argue that there is no universal rational standard of discourse. The fact of moral pluralism in the modern world does not necessarily mean moral chaos. Different societies have different codes by which such virtues as justice, courage and honesty are expressed, but that does not mean that there is a complete mutual incomprehension between different societies when referring to them.

3. *'Facts' and policies in the contemporary world*

Because the 'facts' of a problem need to be known and assessed before making ethical decisions, and the acquiring and assessing of them present considerable difficulties, the way in which churches should make statements on social ethics has needed careful thought. Yet however much we stress the prime importance of the role of lay Christians in family, work and civic life, and I do stress it, there is surely a place for corporate guidance by the churches as a help to lay folk in decision making. Certainly the WCC has always assumed this. It is in reflecting on this that the conviction grew among the pioneers of the WCC that church statements are usually better (except in very clear-cut cases) at a middle level between generalities and detailed proposals.

Generalities are uncontentious but they cut little ice because they are non-specific; detailed proposals, arising from the assessment of 'facts' and forecasts of the probable effects of different policies, are contentious because of the inevitable uncertainties involved in both assessment and forecast. It is rare that a clearcut 'gates of Auschwitz' situation arises, where there is only one possible Christian attitude, and any other can be called a heresy.

It was Dr J. H. Oldham who stressed both the importance of the 'lay' role in civic life in the early days of the Ecumenical Movement, and also the importance of this middle level, using the unfortunate term 'middle axioms', which suggests a process of deductive logic which is not at all what is in mind.[6] He referred to them as 'Attempts to define the direction in which a particular state of society Christian faith must express itself. They are not binding for all time, but are provisional definitions of the type of behaviour required of Christians at a given period and in given circumstances.'[7] I myself would say that they are not *binding* at any time, and that the words *must* and *required* are too strong.

They are not a deduction from a basic doctrinal premise, for they involve assessment of empirical evidence, that is to say of facts' and trends. This is constantly misunderstood. 'The Responsible Society' has often been referred to as a middle axiom, but it is not, because it did not go as far as involving any acquisition or assessment of 'facts'. The most that could be said factually about it is that it expresses verbally a permanent insight from Christian theology which might have been expressed differently in a different culture. For the same reason a 'preferential option for the poor' is not a middle axiom.

From time to time there is a passing reference to this middle level in WCC documents, usually with approval but not with understanding. An example is from a book by Koson Krisang, where he says 'It is my personal belief that the early proposal of J. H. Oldham to work out middle axioms or intermediate criteria still has much value today, and that, in fact, we have followed this direction in many other areas of ethical concern.[8]

As an illustration we can take a middle axiom formulated in the immediate post-1945 period: 'Governments should actively maintain full employment.' This was widely accepted in the 'west' at that time. It has some substance, for it has got beyond generalities. But it does not say *how* governments should do this. This would be too detailed, and there could be several different policies which aimed to do it. Now, partly under the influence of the New Right, inflation has been seen by many as the main danger, more than unemployment. The churches have not been so convinced by this that they have formulated a middle axiom to support it, but their querying of it has been mute. They have not faced the issue. They have not examined the contention of some that full employment will never return. What mix of full employment, stable prices and free collective bargaining is desirable at a given time is an issue churches ought to address.

The cogency of middle axioms depends upon the quality of the work put into arriving at them. Was relevant experience drawn on? Was necessary expertise sought? Was it appraised (especially as experts usually differ)? Church endorsement cannot long give an *imprimatur* to shoddy work. Of course any Christian is free to disagree with a middle axiom. Paul Ramsey, as I mentioned in chapter 4, complained that any recommendations by churches which involve some use and interpretation of empirical data 'faulted the conscience' of those who disagreed with it. But this is not so. A middle axiom is not possible unless there is considerable agreement on evidence and its interpretation. What it does is to shift the burden of 'proof' (or rather plausibility) to the objector, and suggest an attitude to a current issue which Christians should take seriously before making up their minds and acting.

If they prove possible middle axioms have several advantages. They guard against Christian archaism. Churches have often been slow to realize the social changes going on around them, and to live in an imaginary present; instead they are induced to look at the actual present. They compel theologians to work with others, for theologians as such have no access to contemporary evidence. They lend themselves to ecumenical work, though they do not require it. They also lend themselves to working with those of other faiths and philosophies, though again they do not require it. They give the churches something of substance to contribute to public discussion. They can alert society to issues where it is blind or bland. And they guard against the tendency too easily to support the *status quo*, which has been so characteristic in church history. Certainly the whole process is untidy and provisional, needing constant review, but no alternatives have fewer disadvantages. The untidiness of life has to be lived with, and is rarely able to be resolved into unambiguous clarity.

There is, of course, nothing to stop churches going beyond middle axioms into precise details if there is general agreement. Some years ago the call to disinvest in South Africa came near to that. I myself had reservations about this, as to its practicability, and whether the probable secondary consequences of doing so had been sufficiently thought out. But I was grateful for the work put into the question and, in so far as I was in a minority, I did not feel my conscience was faulted; and that was on a detailed policy, not a middle axiom. The South African situation has now passed.

But what if no middle axiom can be reached because of irreconcilable differences of opinion on relevant 'facts' and forecasts. These may well arise because of ideological differences.[9] When it is evident that there is such a conflict of opinion that no agreed middle level conclusion can be reached, it will probably be possible to isolate the chief different approaches and interpretations of evidence, ask the proponents of each to state their position as clearly as they can, and then ask adherents of the other positions questions which they ought to face, and to respond after facing them. Adherents of each position should do the same. Thus each of the most plausible stances that Christians take can be clarified, and so can the questions which other Christians want to put to them. This might seem a meagre harvest from Christian corporate reflection, but it is in fact very important. It does justice to the ambiguities in ethical issues, it takes seriously the necessity for Christians to think through them, and it also takes seriously fellow Christians who come to different conclusions. It is an effort to refine Christian judgments within the body of Christ.[10]

In this book I am concerned with the social witness of the church in the Ecumenical Movement especially as represented by the WCC. I have considered reports, consultations and resolutions. However, there are other ways of witness. Symbolic actions have been mentioned. The Programme to Combat Racism is an example. There is scope for pressure groups by minorities within churches who are convinced of the importance of some line of policy and want to convert the majority to their view. Church

Action on Poverty and Christian pacifist groups are examples. Also some radically-minded Christians have always cropped up in the course of church history who have established separate communities of corporate living as a sharper witness to the Kingdom of God than the more muffled witness of the 'great church'. In some ways their stance is less ambiguous than that of the majority, in other ways it is still ambiguous as it is almost impossible for such communities to cut themselves off from the surrounding civil society, and they exist because that society tolerates them. Pacifist communities are a good example. The story of them, their strengths and limitations, is of great interest. To consider them further would take me too far afield. But wherever possible churches and civil society should find a place for them as part of the total Christian witness.

These problems of theological method have not been explicitly examined in recent years within the WCC. Different groups have favoured a variety of approaches. The Vancouver request for a study of a 'vital and coherent theology' was a recognition of the variety of approaches, which cause confusion because they are unexamined. The confusion continues and has not diminished.

4. *Risk assessment and risk taking*

Since an element in decision making in social ethics is an estimate of the likely effects of different possible policy options, this immediately raises the question of risk assessment. The longer the time span we have in mind the greater are the difficulties it presents. There is a fair amount of secular literature on the matter, but very little Christian discussion.[11]

What is our obligation to future generations? Are they to count as neighbours to be loved as we love ourselves? They are human beings who do not yet exist, with whom we can have no reciprocal relationship. They have no vote. Personal and collective long-term moral responsibility is a relatively new ethical issue as our technical powers and global knowledge have increased so dramatically. How far ahead should we look? Most people on reflection would probably say as long as we can reasonably foresee; perhaps as far as our grandchildren. But that raises problems. Markets left to themselves have hardly more than ten years in perspective. Many major technical advances which have had widespread social and cultural effects were not foreseen twenty-five years ago. On the other hand we have created the problem of disposing of radioactive nuclear waste with a half life of many thousands of years. Again most people, on reflection, would probably say we should foreclose issues as little as possible, especially if some irreversible environmental factor is involved. As far as possible we should leave all the options open for future generations. In all this I am not aware of any insights peculiar to Christianity, which are not shared widely by those who have thought about it.

Problems of forecasting can be briefly illustrated by issues of climate and energy. There are many uncertainties in forecasting the effect of human activity on climate. We are not sure whether clouds have a heating or cooling effect. And the upper layers of the sea are an enormous heat sink, so that the full effects of the greater discharge of greenhouse gases into the atmosphere in raising the temperature will be delayed. I am no expert in this field. The impression I get (as I have already mentioned) is that the slow effect of human activity which has already taken place will probably raise the temperature by 1°c by the year 2025. We have time to deal with the forseeable consequences of this, and there will be gainers and losers, but we need to get on with it. If we want to prevent a further increase of temperature after 2025 we have to begin now because social policies in this area take about thirty years to work out, and have to be internationally determined. On energy requirements the projections are very uncertain. Those projections made in 1972 about USA energy requirements in 1983 were 60% too high; and global projections of energy use in the year 2050 vary from one third to four times the present level. Uncertainty about population growth is related to this. Demographers have continually to revise their forecasts, for the factors which affect the rate at which human beings decide to reproduce themselves remain very mysterious. Some factors are known; I have already mentioned the education of girls. But at least we are sure that population will grow, and more in the 'south' than the 'north'. The poor in the 'south' will be the principal sufferers.

Weighing risks is tricky. For instance, how do we weigh the

benefits of a *possible*, but uncertain, catastrophe in the future against *certain* costs now? An entirely safety-first policy would appear to be timid. In moral theology it is called tutiorism, and is condemned as an unsuitable criterion for Christian living. On the other hand we have to watch lest after waiting until the evidence is unambiguous we find it is too late to act. The question of pollution raises rather similar issues. The costs of reducing it are now and the benefits in the future. Or in the case of the disposal of radio active waste and the development of nuclear fusion (should it prove commercially possible), depend on maintaining relatively stable social institutions and constant vigilance indefinitely. If one doubts the feasibility of this there is the evidence of the dykes in the Netherlands. They require perpetual vigilance or a large area of that country would be flooded in depth. So far vigilance has been maintained. However, if we try to make the vigilance routine, even though technically sophisticated, there is the danger that on occasion humans may fail out of boredom in carrying out routine maintenance.

On most of these issues long-term international co-operation is needed. It is painfully slow and hard to secure. The Rio summit was a beginning. A strong argument on national self interest lines has to be mounted to persuade nations to co-operate, and especially the rich and powerful to support the poorer and populous. For example, we have seen that unless support is forthcoming China and India can subvert the plan to abolish the use of chlorofluorocarbons.

If Christian opinion is to be alerted on these matters much more work has to be done. So far the WCC has done very little to illuminate the problems of risk assessment. The only place known to me where it has been taken up is in one section of the conference at the Massachusetts Institute of Technology in 1979.[12] However, one thing is clear. Those who favour eschatological realism, and who stress the apocalyptic vision of the new things God will bring about, unrelated to present trends, are not sympathetic to issues of risk assessment.[13] They have a strong tendency to take a worst case analysis of the present, to jump to the demand for a totally new order, and to find a foretaste of it in local grass roots communities which are held to be the power base 'from below' of the future. They do not make a contribution to the issues I have been discussing. They want an unambiguous Christian position, when the real problem is how to achieve greater clarity and at the same time to live with some confidence amid the inevitable ambiguities, and the differences of opinion which result from coming to grips with these pressing large-scale issues.

10 Looking to the Future in Ecumenical Social Ethics

In this last chapter I begin by a return to the whole context of the Ecumenical Movement, which is where I began, and where social theology and ethics finds its plan. After that I attempt to focus more sharply on present defects in its procedures and contents, and then consider prospects for the work now planned to lead up to the next Assembly, and fiftieth anniversiay of the WCC, at Harare in 1998.

1. *The ecumenical stalemate*

Ecumenism has without doubt lost impetus at a confessional level. Some serious and not unfriendly theologians say bluntly that it is dead. Bishop Oliver Tomkins, a leading figure in Faith and Order, said sadly, towards the end of his life, 'Ecumenism now sees that churches have no greater courage, love and unselfishness than any other institutions to change structures, relinquish power, and renounce vested interests'. In England the bright hopes for a decisive move towards church unity by Easter Sunday 1980, and even by the year 2000, have vanished. In the Church of England a minority was on two occasions just big enough to prevent the healing of the Anglican-Methodist division at the last stage, and even to block a covenant commitment with the Free Churches. (Ironically the minority was divided into groups which rejected them on mutually incompatible grounds.) Conversation between the Church of England and the Church of Scotland foundered, one reason being the force of Scottish national sentiment and the failure of the English to appreciate the extent of it. On a wider front the promising progress made by the Anglican-Roman Catholic International Commission, remarkable after four hundred years of hostility, has been hindered, though not halted, by the Sacred Congregation for the Defence of the Faith, in Rome. After ten years of pondering on the Final Report of the first ARCIC it produced a cool reply, which 'changed the goalposts' by going back on the premises on which Pope Paul VI and Archbishop Michael Ramsey had set it up. In doing so it ignored the much more positive responses from national Episcopal Conferences which had most experience of Anglicans. Multiply these set-backs on a global scale, with few examples to put against them, and remembering the variety of churches outside the main confessional stream, and often outside the Ecumenical Movement, and it is evident that it has a long way to go.

Of course there are genuine theological differences. But they are bound up in a subtle way with matters of historical memories (which need some purging), and nationalism; to these must be added ecclesiastical power politics. Here the Roman Catholic Church is most conspicuous because of its size and centralization. Its relations with Orthodoxy, with which it is in many ways close, are soured because power struggles down the centuries have notably worsened since the collapse of the USSR. In fact there is a diversity of theological position within all the main confessional traditions, and since it is obvious that what divides Christians is far less than what they have in common, a strong conviction of the need for unity could move the process on. This is the more possible in that we now see how much divisions in the past were caused by cultural factors and power politics. The problem is to generate the will to overcome present institutional obstacles. Here the Roman Catholic Church is of key importance. To an outsider it seems that the Curia must be reformed. What was intended as an executive agency has become a dominant policy-making one, in a centralization which can be helpful but may well be injurious to churches in different parts of the world. But of course the Pope himself is of decisive importance. John XXIII, against all expectations, began a shake-up (*aggiornamento*). We must hope for another leader to continue it. There are grounds for thinking that had John Paul I not died so suddenly he would have done so. The hopeful feature is that at local level relations are better than they have ever been down the centuries, and very many are now ready for initiatives from the top, when they were not ready for those of John XXIII.

Faced with this situation, many in the WCC, including some at the highest level, are disposed to give up the quest for church unity as hopeless, and to turn to more local and informal sources of renewal; to unofficial groups when official ones have become frozen. I do not think Faith and Order will let this happen. It will go on preparing the ground for a new move forward, confident that the day will come, probably in as surprising a way as it did with John XXIII. It is fortified in this by the manifest loss of influence of divided churches in Europe, the heartland of Christianity from the early centuries until recently. The omnicompetent church is increasingly rejected by those under the age of fifty, whilst churches which make fewer overall claims are becoming marginalized in a privatization of faith. All churches need a competent social theology and ethics.

A co-chair person of the European Values Study has written of the Roman Catholic Church, 'Too many paragraphs of the new *Catechism of the Roman Catholic Church* speak as if there had been no serious studies of scripture since the beginning of the century, as if there had been no movement for women's emancipation, and as if the teaching of *Humanae Vitae* had been wholeheartedly received by the faithful and bishops.' He goes on to say that human rights have come to the fore everywhere in 'western' public life, but discussion of the implications for the institutional Catholic Church itself is taboo. There are strands of a similar attitude to the Bible and to tradition in other churches. And all churches need to listen to those who, for reasons of individual honesty, live on the periphery of the church, or who have left the church and become 'homeless' Christians. The same writer concludes, 'Only ecumenical initiatives hold out the promise that Christianity will have a greater influence in European culture at the turn of the millennium than it does now.'[1]

The churches could in fact go a lot further together than they do, even under the present constrictions. They could seriously ask themselves the question put at the Lund Faith and Order Conference in 1952: 'Should not our churches ask themselves whether they are showing sufficient eagerness to enter into conversation with other churches and *whether they should not act together in all matters except those in which deep differences of conviction compel them to act separately*.' One example is that they could develop to its maximum potential our common baptism, which nearly all Christian churches accept. It would surely help in Northern Ireland if the churches worked towards a situation where a Roman Catholic was present at Protestant and Anglican baptisms, and *vice versa*. There is no theological obstacle or church rule to prevent it.

Europe, however, is only one continent with which the WCC and the Roman Catholic Church are concerned. What are the special problems of the WCC? I summarize. Its size, and the variety of contexts represented, lead to a vast agenda, fissiparousness and mediocrity; also to an enhanced role for its staff. The attempt within the staff to be representative of area, sex, confessional tradition – and even of causes – means that it is not all of the highest quality. Yet the WCC can only survive by excellence. With its vast potential it ought to be a little ahead of member churches, and something of a challenge to them. But it cannot be too far ahead or it will not be listened to. It is *not* basically a frontier movement (in sociological terms), as some of its leaders like to think, but it can illuminate frontiers if it differentiates clearly between Consultations, which speak *to* the churches, and which can feed Assemblies, which speak *for* the churches (subject to the provisions of the Toronto Statement). Since about 1970 the WCC has not reflected sufficiently on its role, and that of the churches, as change agents or conservers, as catalysts or inhibitors of change.

The tendency in recent years has been to promote in social ethics a premature consensus, based upon an implicit theology, and an analysis of the data of current issues which is congenial to it. In so far as experts are called in they are ones who support the analysis which suits the theology. Other representative theologies and analyses are not represented; dialogue between them is not promoted. This is in sharp contrast to the way Faith and Order has always proceeded. I discuss this further in the next section.

2. *Defects in recent ecumenical social ethics: A summary*

The WCC mounts a formidable attack on the evils of the modern world. There is no lack of them. And the Christian gospel gives us strong grounds for condemning humanly-made corruptions and

injustices. As distinct from previous centuries, modern communications make us instantly aware of them globally. It is a burden
which we have to learn to carry. It becomes inhibiting if we slide
into thinking that our sorry state of affairs is worse than in
previous ages. Life for the majority of human beings throughout
history has been nasty, poor, brutish and short (to quote part of a
phrase of Thomas Hobbes in the seventeenth century), but it was
not known globally. This may partly be why the WCC tends to
look on the worst side, take a worst case analysis, and then
demand a total transformation of social, economic and political
institutions (with occasional sentences cropping up suggesting that
it does not really mean this, but rather a reform of them, the
details of such a reform not being stated).

Dramatic statements may be used as a shock tactic. 'The world
is a Titanic on a collision course', said a main speaker at the
Nairobi Assembly. This has its place. But the effect of shock
statements wears off by their constant use. Such language is often
used of ecological apocalyptic vision of a new state for humanity
and creation, which God will bring about. Those who emphasize
this apocalyptic biblical vision do not bring it alongside our
present scientific understanding of the universe. We do not know
whether or not the expansive force of the 'big bang', which is
driving the galaxies apart, will prevail over the contracting force
of gravity, which is pulling them together. If the former is the
stronger the galaxies will go on receding from one another, and
gradually within each galaxy matter will disappear through
condensation into black holes. If the latter force prevails, gravity
will in due course reverse the expansion of galaxies and matter
will return to its original concentration. The time scale is in tens of
billions of years. We do not know whether the process will then
be repeated. (We do not know whether there are other universes.)
In either case human existence will cease long before the process
does. We are a very transient feature of the universe. But in the
Christian understanding of creation we are central to it. Yet
human fulfilment being so obviously incomplete in our brief span
of life, miserably constricted as it has been, and is, for most
humans, Christians trust that God's faithfulness will complete in
us what he has begun. The resurrection of Jesus, which can be
understood in various ways, is a sign of this. A non-realist God,

who is a projection of human aspirations, which are then fortified by dwelling on Christian 'stories', is a noble form of belief, as was Stoicism in the Graeco-Roman world, but it will not do as a version of Christian belief. It is a Christian atheism. But like other atheisms it may have the effect of purifying inadequate theology.

It can agree with Christian theism in making some fundamental affirmations about human life, such as the dignity of the human person (however flawed a person may be). The language of 'we affirm', 'we commit', 'we resist' (I am quoting from the Seoul Convocation) is appropriate at this basic level. Problems come with moving to specific issues, as chapter 9 in particular discussed. There is a marked strain in some Protestant theologies which is reluctant to engage in practical moral reasoning involving empirical data, for fear that the uncertainties revealed will inhibit whole hearted devotion to living by the gospel. Hence the appeal to an intuitive approach to decision making. There is a tendency in Lutheranism to regard such efforts of the practical reason as a form of 'works righteousness', trying to make oneself acceptable to God by moral efforts rather than relying on faith alone. The usefulness of general moral reasoning is thus denied in favour of saying that obedience to what God requires can only be known in the immediate context of decisions.[2] It is one form of Situationism. It is such influences as these which may lie behind much of the dominant strain in WCC social ethics. No one would say it should not be represented, and taken seriously; but it should not have a near monopoly.

There is a link between these tendencies and a desire to stress what is distinctively Christian in ethics, which has led to a recent emphasis on an ethic of virtue, formed within the Christian congregation, and nourished by the Christian narrative. Separatist and sectarian conclusions can be drawn from this, but need not be. When they are, there is an abjuring of responsibility for macro policies in the public realm, and from direct responsibility for a common human flourishing (apart from the indirect influence of authentic Christian communal life),[3] leaving the rest to God. In some situations of extreme pressure on Christians this may be the best, perhaps the only, possible course. It is Richard Niebuhr's 'Christ Against Culture' position. But it is odd to adopt it in 'liberal' societies, which allow the conditions which make such a stand relatively easy, whilst castigating the liberalism which does so. This attitude is a possible influence on the dominant WCC stance.

This stance also tends to lead to utopian attitudes, policies and strategies. As an example of utopian strategies the Seoul Convocation actually said that church representatives should report back to the Canberra Assembly, only ten months later, on what actions their churches had taken on its commitments. As an example of an utopian policy, it wanted a new economic order not based on profits (showing that it had not grasped the rudiments of serious economic reflection); and the abolition of war from international relations. The various experts at Seoul were not used, and remained in helpless frustration in the midst of these simplicities, from which, whatever defects experts may be liable to, they might have saved it.[4]

The simplicity in thought with regard to international affairs has continued. The Unit III Committee, which is responsible for the programme with the revised title 'Theology of Life: Justice, Peace and Creation', proposed parallel to it a 'Programme to Overcome Violence'. This was accepted by the Central Committee at its meeting in Johannesburg in 1994. Both will run until the next Assembly, in Harare in 1988. The resolution speaks of the need to overcome the spirit, logic and practice of war, and says, 'This may indeed be a time when the churches together should face the challenge to give up any theological or other justification of the use of military power, and to become a *koinonia* dedicated to the pursuit of a just peace'. This is very similar to the resolution introduced by Konrad Raiser at the Canberra Assembly, which was passed one day and rescinded the next, when its implications were realized.

If one is a pacifist on theological grounds the resolution makes sense; if not it does not. The phrase 'just peace' is a playing with words. To begin with, no difference is made between violence and force. Violence refers to a use of force which is to be condemned. Force is essential to human flourishing. It is related to law and order, which has to be scrutinized for abuses, but which has to be upheld to avoid anarchy. Violence may be either a corruption of law and order by oppressors or an act of the oppressed against injustice. Force needs to be brought under the rule of law; the Just War tradition can be brought to bear on questions of force in relation to law and order. It is still valid when wrestling with issues of war. It is not a question of abolishing military power, which is a necessity under God for whatever unit constitutes the basic civil authority (we have no reason to suppose it must always be that relative newcomer, the nation state), to maintain justice in the service of love. Justice and peace may therefore, alas, conflict. We have painfully to work at the conditions under which military power is permissible, and the ways in which it can legitimately be used (that is to say *ad bellum* and *in bello*). The very slow advances in International Law show how difficult this is, but there is no way of avoiding it.

The recent work of the WCC is seriously flawed by its tendency not just to be critical of the misuse of power, but suspicious of any actual use of it, including the place of power in international relations. There is the suggestion that the powerlessness of the cross negates all power in human life. This ignores the 'Two Realms' in which Christians live. Christian pacifists do think like this, but they have never convinced most Christians that this is what love requires. They should certainly be heard, but it is disastrous if the WCC adopts their position, tacitly or explicitly. A firmer theology is needed.

That firmer theology will also be relevant to the action-reflection model in social ethics. It has tended to be a one-way traffic, with theology always lagging behind, to support the actions. It has been put forward to express commitment to the marginalized and to regard anything else as elitist. But *uncritical* preoccupation with the marginalized will lead to the marginalization of the WCC itself.

The firmer theology must not be one-dimensional. In the 'Integrity of Creation' studies there have been demands for a holistic theology and an end of dualism. The WCC has not been alone in this. It has followed a strong movement among a section of 'western' intellectuals in the last quarter of a century. But instead of bringing a theological critique to bear on it, the WCC has uncritically endorsed it, and not tried to bring it into dialogue with other theologies. Opposition to dualism has led to the demand for the distinction between God and nature, or humanity and nature, or this world and 'the next' to be abolished or blurred. There are great dangers here. The opposite of dualism, metaphysically, is monism. Societies which have merged humans into nature have been static and restrictive. God's transcendence needs stressing, and so does the unity of humanity under God. Human persons are constituted by their relation to other persons and not by subsuming them with plants and animals. Human moral issues are not to be reduced to questions of ecology so that nature is on an equal footing with human society, or is even pictured as standing in judgment over it. Indeed human issues must not be reasoned about in a way which puts the natural sciences, or one of them (for example ecology) in a position of intellectual supremacy. This is an abdication of the role of theology. True, it cannot be any longer the 'queen of the sciences'. It cannot dominate them, but neither can it be forced into an intellectual straitjacket by them. By all means let the WCC promote a dialogue between antidualist and dualist theologies, but not follow uncritically the antidualist one.[5]

Behind it has been the uncritical acceptance of an ecological cosmology according to which the earth is seen as a vast interlocking system in which no part should be isolated from the rest. Behind the 'Theology of Life' programme there is an utopian view of nature which totally ignores conflicts in it within the evolutionary process, and today. (This is akin to the ignoring of the conflicts of life with life in human society, because of an unreal attitude to power.) This type of thinking is also probably behind the underplaying of population problems in the 'two thirds world'. The essence of it is that any economic improvement is likely to be negated by the growth of population.

Similar problems arise in economic analysis. Statements from the WCC, and books which it publishes, and thereby to which it gives a certain approval, are dominated by a hostility to a more global economy which is free from the restrictions which the GATT negotiations have striven to overcome, in favour of a more nationalist orientation that seeks to concentrate on production for internal national markets, and after that, as a second best, regional self-sufficiency. The question of international trade comes last. There are a few eco-economists who take this line, but the vast majority of economists, speaking as *pure* economists, would emphasize the very great reduction in the productivity of relatively

scarce resources this would entail; and speaking as *political* economists would point out the dangers of this stress on nationalism
and the nation state. Clearly both positions need scrutiny. But the
WCC expert advisers in this area appear to be predominantly
from the small band of eco-economists. There is no presentation
of the other view.

There is connected with this an attempt to maintain that there
is an ecumenical consensus on economic and environmental issues.
In so far as there appears to be one it has been achieved by exclu-
sion. This is a departure from the way ecumenical work in social
ethics was started, and which has always been pursued by
Faith and Order. Without willingness to recognize differences
as frankly as agreements the WCC would never have got started.
In ignorance of, or disregarding in social ethics, the Toronto
Statement's foundation principles the WCC has overlooked the
fact that it should be a forum for examining disagreements, with
the aim of clarifying them, and if possible modifying or resolving
them. Christian unity does not mean ideological conformity or
political solidarity. We have been presented with inadequate
dialogue, analyses and proposals. A better theological method
would show that there are disagreements on data and policies
between those who are agreed on doctrine, or agreements on data
and analysis between those who disagree on doctrine, or disagreements on both. This is the context in which the parameters of
unity and renewal are to be explored.

A greater ecumenical memory is needed. If Roman Catholic
social theology is constricted by too great a dependence on the
traditional deposit of teaching, ecumenical social theology rides
too loosely to it. Work in previous decades on the human, and on
the place of the secular (as against secularism as an ideology)
needs bringing alongside current preoccupations. Concern on this
point has recently been expressed by the informal group of friends
of the WCC, referred to in chapter 4, which met three times from
1990.[6] I was a member of that group, but in this book I represent
only myself. My plea is that the group's criticisms be taken
seriously. My argument needs sifting in an ecumenical process.
My own conviction, to put it bluntly, is that Christians from the
First World need to speak up more. As I have said, at present the
bitterness of the Third World is met by the guilt of the First

which, because of its wealth and power, has the greater responsibility. Hence it finds it difficult to speak frankly of some simplistic analyses, and some unfortunate political practices that come from the Third World. How is it possible to marry the concerns of the Third World with the 'expertise' of the First? To quote from a private paper, 'It is true that starving people know hunger in a way that no clinician can know it. But the experience of hunger does not itself provide the agricultural, dietary, economic and political skills that produce and distribute food.' In an ecumenical fellowship a higher quality of dialogue and mutual correction should be possible. Those of the 'west' ought to have their complacencies exposed, and at the same time advance considerations which their intellectual integrity demands.

After the first meeting of the group it addressed an Open Letter to Emilio Castro, who was then General Secretary of the WCC, expressing its concerns. He referred to it in his report to the Canberra Assembly. He misunderstood it as a call to moderation rather than to taking sides. On the contrary, he said, the WCC 'dares to say a word that calls to action and support those who act, and that there is a lesser risk in this than that of a neutrality or passiveness which borders on indifference'. The prophets of the Old Testament received a precise summons to 'speak'; and when the ecumenical community speaks it has the advantage that what it says comes out of a dialogical situation, and in particular of participation with those who suffer in their local situation.[7]

This raises such questions as (1) Did the Open Letter advocate neutrality or passivity? (2) What does it mean to be prophetic? (3) The respective roles of advocacy and education in the WCC. (4) Is the WCC adequately in dialogue and with whom? (5) Granted that it pays particular attention to those who suffer, and to being alongside then, does this mean that their opinion of what should be done, as distinct from their account of their sufferings, must necessarily be accepted?

This book has tried to deal with such questions and to show that Emilio Castro's reply was inadequate. What hope is there of a more adequate response from the WCC as its study programme begins the run up to the next Assembly in 1998? And what hope is there of more fruitful relations with the Vatican in work in the area of social theology and ethics?

3. *The new programme and the possibilities of reform*

The possibilities of reform in working at ecumenical social ethics do not in the first instance seem encouraging. As far as Roman Catholic work is concerned it looks as if things will go on much as they are now, as far as we can immediately foresee. *Veritatis Splendor* will not bring the internal debate in that church to an end. It may be muted, under pressure from Rome, or it may be exacerbated. Co-operation between the Vatican and the WCC will continue in its present cautiously restricted form. Neither side will wish to take the responsibility for ending it. Whether either can learn from the other remains to be seen. Recent Roman Catholic work in the economic area has been better researched than that of the WCC, but in many social and political areas the felt need to defend the conclusions and method of reasoning in *Humanae Vitae* on population issues is a serious handicap to the credibility of the Vatican, and to ecumenical co-operation in social ethics. Whether the Roman Catholic Church can bring itself to admit diversity of opinion within itself, and so liberate it for more fruitful work with others, I cannot tell. As one who has learned a great deal from Roman Catholic Moral Theology, and from friendship with Roman Catholic Moral Theologians, I strongly hope so. But I am not a skilled Vatican watcher.

From the side of the WCC the new programme 'A Theology of Life: Justice, Peace and Creation', is at least as vast as before, and backed up by analyses which so far are just as monolithic and simplistic. The Central Committee, elected at Canberra, with many new members, seems unlikely to have enough talent, experience and cohesion to monitor closely this programme, and could easily be carried away by a largely staff-propelled enterprise. Any reformed procedure would have to be generated 'in house'. Again the omens are not good. In 1991 Konrad Raiser, who has since become General Secretary, wrote a book *Ecumenism in Transition*.[8] In it he distances himself from the tradition of the Ecumenical Movement in both Life and Work and Faith and Order. Previous stress on the Mosaic Covenant, salvation history, universalism, and secularization as a fruit of the biblical witness is 'western' and triumphalist, based on a 'christology from above'. Now we need to work on a 'christology from below'. This sees

God in history as revolutionary, not evolutionary, involving human solidarity, not dominion, and a new attitude to other religions. This last point is well taken. However, the Social Trinity is stressed, and the human correspondence drawn from it is a fellowship of men and women without privileges and without sub-jugation, as if this Trinitarian model (itself not satisfactory unless corrected by other models) could be directly transferred to the church, which is a body of forgiven sinners who never get beyond all need of forgiveness. This picture of an unstructured fellowship cannot be applied directly to the church; still less to the institu-tions of family, work and State. It is also said that talk of a conciliar fellowship has to be given up, because there is no hope of a universal Council; but we are able to talk of a conciliar process.

On this last point it is rather a *pre*-conciliar process, as I have already mentioned, because Roman Catholics, Orthodox and others find it hard to see how non-church groups, who are involved in the outreaches of the Life and Work side, can be part of a conciliar process of churches. But leaving that aside the general picture drawn from *Ecumenism in Transition* is not encouraging from my point of view. For the rest the book reflects attitudes which I have already queried, such as a distrust of the use of secular power, and neglect of conserving role for the churches. Its tendency to abandon Faith and Order pre-occupations as hopeless, and to subsume them under the general struggles of the oppressed of humanity against their oppressors smacks too much of the collapsed Marxist theories.

A key issue is whether the Seoul process and its results can be questioned. It epitomizes the weakness of recent WCC social theo-logy and ethics. So far it is always represented as significant, and broadly a success. The WCC is reluctant to admit a failure here, as is the Vatican to admit one with *Humanae Vitae*. This is crucial for the 'Theology of Life' programme. Will the unsatisfactoriness of the preparatory process, the marginalization of the expert consultants at the Convocation, the unreality of the massiveness of the programme, and the banality of some of the ten affirmations which emerged, be open to question? Or will it continue to be heralded as a significant event, setting the tone and content of work until 1998?

The attempt to regard it as a beacon for Faith and Order does not augur well. In preparation for the conference of Faith and Order at Compestala in north west Spain in 1993, a joint Consultation was held in the spring of that year in Denmark between the Faith and Order and Life and Work sides of the WCC, on 'Koinonia and Justice, Peace and the Integrity of Creation'. Its report is being treated as the lynchpin of the integration of the work of the WCC.[9] The Report contains some good points, such as its discussion of the problem of differentiating the global from the local, and preventing the latter degenerating into tribalism (par. 35–8). The stress on *koinonia* ethics is also promising for there has been lately a Post-modernist stress on the ambivalent and the indeterminate, as against unity and coherence. Community has been described as a 'tetrasyllabic mouthful attached to everything and signifying nothing'. Against this *koinonia* has in English the sense of communion, fellowship and participation, with *diakonia* (service) as its corollary. The WCC does well to pursue this theme and to stress mutual accountability, not letting this be lost in contextualism.

However there are serious weaknesses in the Report, because it takes the Justice, Peace and Integrity of Creation process as beyond criticism. The Faith and Order folk at the Consultation were clearly not sufficiently *au fait* to challenge it. The claim is made that that the process has brought fresh light and energy to the ecumenical scene, and that it marks a new ecumenical beginning (par. 24). Indeed the being (*esse*) of the church is at stake in it (par. 6). Its concept of covenanting may actually be a help to Faith and Order. The Seoul Convocation is assumed to have been a success, and its Ten Affirmations to constitute an ecumenical catechism (par. 52 and Appendix 1). All this seems to me a delusion. There is indeed a section on different analyses and responses, and a criticism of a tendency to canonize one point of view and reject others (par. 51), a welcome note. An important point on which it is unclear is how far a *koinonia* ethic is distinctively Christian and how far it overlaps with that of other faiths and philosophies (paras 24, 44, 45). This in turn is connected to how the church sees itself in relation to 'the world'.

The prevailing tendency of the Report is a ringing endorsement of the 'Justice, Peace and Integrity of Creation' process as a help to the processes of Faith and Order. I think the reverse is the case.

If the Faith and Order method is not followed by the Life and Work side it will continue in futility.

The next few years will tell. The 'Theology of Life' programme could reform itself. There is no barrier to prevent it. If not the WCC will cast away its unique potentiality for being a help and challenge to the churches. That is what it was in its early days. Now it is not. I quote from a paper written for the meeting at Bossey in February 1994 by Professor Roger Shinn, formerly of Union Theological Seminary, New York:

> Those of us who are frequently called to defend the WCC from critics are embarrassed by the combination of dogmatism and carelessness that marks too much of the literature of the WCC. Too many loyal Christians are saying that they can make their witness elsewhere better than through the WCC. Too many secular observers are brushing aside our declarations as they did not in the days of Karl Barth, Reinhold Niebuhr, Barbara Ward, T.P. Simatupang and Margaret Mead. We had our vicious critics then, but we were not embarrassed by what the WCC said. I do not suggest that we idealize some Golden Age. In many ways we have surpassed our forerunners, in openness to new currents in the world's cultures and our ecological sensitivities. But I wish we could emulate the best wisdom of our past as we break new ground.[10]

Notes

Part One: Past and Present

Introduction: A Preliminary Sketch – The ABC of the WCC

1. As a young man I was joint secretary of the Youth section of the Oxford Conference of 1937 on 'Church Community and State'. Since then I have been in fairly close touch with the heart of the operations of the WCC without ever being part of it, except for seven months in 1969 when I was seconded to take temporary charge of the Church and Society unit, with which I have had a long continued association until the late 1980s. For several years between 1970 and 1980 I ran a third year special option in Ecumenical Social Ethics in the Honours Degree in Theology at Manchester University.

2. *Dictionary of the Ecumenical Movement*, ed. Nicholas Lossky, Jose Miguel Bonino, John S. Pobee, Thomas Stransky, Geoffrey Wainwright, and Pauline Webb, WCC, Geneva and the Council of Churches for Britain and Ireland, London 1991. This contains as much information as most general enquirers will need in its comprehensive range, whilst references to follow up particular entries in more detail are given.

3. See the *Dictionary of the Ecumenical Movement*, passim.

4. The first four Councils (Nicea 325, Constantinople 381, Ephesus 481, and Chalcedon 451) are recognized by nearly all 'mainline' churches. The Orthodox and Roman Catholics recognize three more (553, 650 and 787), and Roman Catholics recognize fourteen more, the most well known being Trent (1545–63), Vatican I (1870), and Vatican II (1962–65). The Nicene Creed is really that of the Council of Constantinople (381); mainstream churches which do not, or do not often, use it in their eucharistic liturgies, have it in the background as a norm.

5. Hans Küng, *Global Responsibility*, SCM Press and Crossroad Publishing 1991.

6. There are churches which are beyond the bounds of 'normative' Christianity, because they accept key texts in addition to the Bible, like

Christian Science (Mr Baker Eddy's *Science and Health: the key to the Scriptures*), or Mormons (*The Book of Mormon*). Jehovah's Witness, though biblically based, does not claim to be Christian.

7. T. C. Chao of China, elected one of the six Presidents of the WCC at Amsterdam, resigned when the Central Committee at Toronto in 1950 supported the United Nations 'police action' against the invasion by North Korea of South Korea.

8. I was a member of a group which met in Vancouver in 1990, Berlin in 1992 and Manchester in 1993 to clarify this criticism. After Vancouver an Open Letter was sent to the then General Secretary of the WCC, Emilio Castro; after Berlin a pamphlet was produced, 'The Future of Ecumenical Social Thought'; after Manchester a letter was sent by the Archbishop of York, who chaired the group, to the new General Secretary, Konrad Raiser (see chapter 4).

1. *An Outline of Ecumenical Social Ethics 1: From its Roots to 1966*

1. The standard histories of the Ecumenical Movement and the WCC are *A History of the Ecumenical Movement 1517–1948*, ed. Ruth Rouse and Stephen C. Neill, SPCK 1954, 2nd ed. WCC 1986, and *The Ecumenical Advance: a History of the Ecumenical Movement 1948–1968*, ed. Harold E. Fey, WCC 1970 and 1986. A key account of events up to 1950 is W.A. Visser 't Hooft, *The Genesis and Formation of the World Council of Churches*, WCC, Geneva 1982. *The Dictionary of the Ecumenical Movement* (see note 2 to the introductory chapter) is indispensable for the years after 1948. As far as social theology and ethics is specifically concerned there is Edward Duff, *The Social Thought of the World Council of Churches*, Longmans Green 1956. There is a large literature on particular aspect of the work of the WCC, and various consultations, and perhaps the most useful sources are two issues of *The Ecumenical Review*, the quarterly journal of the WCC, 'Church and Society: Ecumenical Perspective: Essays in Honour of Paul Abrecht', vol. 37, no. 1 January 1985, and 'Fifty Years of Ecumenical Social Thought', vol. 40, no. 2 April 1988.

2. Cf. *The Stockholm Conference 1925*, ed. G. K. A. Bell, OUP 1925.

3. Cf. W. A. Visser 't Hooft and J. H. Oldham, *The Church and its Function in Society*, Allen & Unwin 1937, and *The Churches Survey their Task, the Report of the Conference at Oxford on Church, Community and State*, Allen & Unwin 1937. The six volumes of essays were issued by the same publisher in 1937, and details can be found in the front of the Conference Report volume.

4. Cf. W. A. Visser 't Hooft *Memoirs*, SCM Press 1973.

5. Cf. *The First Assembly of the World Council of Churches*, *Amsterdam*, ed. W. A. Visser 't Hooft, Harper, New York 1949: Walter Muildu, *Foundation of a Responsible Society*, Abingdon Press, Nashville 1959; Paul Bock, *In Search of a Responsible Society; The Social Teachings of the World Council of Churches*, Westminster Press, Philadelphia 1974.

6. Asians did make use of the term in a report 'The Responsible Society in Asian Perspective' (1959). It was specifically challenged in a chapter by Richard Shaull 'Revolutionary Change in Theological Perspective' in the preparatory volume for the Geneva Conference *Christian Social Ethics in a Changing World* (see chapter 2, note 3).

7. Cf. Paul Abrecht, *The Churches and Rapid Social Change*, SCM Press 1961, and Egbert de Vries, *Man in Rapid Social Change*, SCM Press 1961.

2. *An Outline of Ecumenical Social Ethics 2: From 1966*

1. The Russians were at a disadvantage because of the very few from other countries who understood Russian. They made it worse by sending delegates who could not understand any of the other four 'western' languages. It was thought that interpreters who accompanied them, on whom they were dependent, were government officials.

2. Particularly certain passages from *Letters and Papers from Prison*, ET, third revised and enlarged edition, SCM Press 1967.

3. The Geneva volumes were *Christian Social Ethics in a Changing World: an Ecumenical Theological Enquiry*, ed. John C. Bennett; *Responsible Government in a Revolutionary Age*, ed. Z. K. Matthews; *Economic Growth in World Perspective*, ed. Denys Munby; *Man in Community: Christian Concern for the Human in Changing Society*, ed. Egbert de Vries (all SCM Press 1966).

4. I discussed these and other matters connected with the organization of Geneva in chapter 1 of a symposium *Technology and Social Justice: an International Symposium on the Social and Economic Teaching of the WCC from Geneva 1966 to Uppsala 1968*, SCM Press 1971, which I edited. Regrettably it is still relevant; there is no easy solution to the problems it discusses.

5. (*a*) The Statements of the Zagorsk Consultation on 'Theological Issues of Church and Society' can be found in *Study Encounter*, Vol.IV, no. 2 1968, WCC, Geneva. (*b*) 'Nature' had not come to the fore as an issue in 1968, but an understanding of the human is central to one's attitude to it, though this is not always recognized by ecologists.

6. Cf. *Theology of Hope; On the Ground and Implications of a Christian Eschatology*, ET SCM Press 1967; also many subsequent books by Moltmann.

7. Cf. 'Violence, Non-violence and the Struggle for Justice', WCC, Geneva 1973, and 'Violence, Non-violence and Civil Conflict', WCC, Geneva 1983.

8. Cf. Darril Hudson, *The Ecumenical Movement in World Affairs*, Weidenfeld & Nicholson 1969, and Ans J. Van der Bent, *Christian Response in a World of Crisis; A Brief History of the WCC's Commission of the Churches on International Affairs*, WCC, Geneva 1986.

9. 'Ecumenical Perspectives on Political Ethics' a consultation organized by the Commission on the Churches' Participation in Development, Cyprus 1981, WCC, Geneva 1983.

10. 'Conscientization' refers to a process of awareness raising whereby the oppressed and marginalized can become subjects of their own history, and not objects controlled by others; cf. Paulo Freire, *Pedagogy of the Oppressed*, Herder, New York 1970.

11. Cf. the theological framework of *Koinonia* in which the Anglican-Roman Catholic International Doctrinal Commission has set its work. An important study on 'Koinonia in Scripture: Survey of Biblical Texts' was produced by John Reumann at the Faith and Order Conference at Santiago de Compostela in Spain, 1993.

12. The two MIT volumes are *Faith and Science in a Unjust World*, Vol. 1 ed. Roger Shinn, Vol. 2 ed. Paul Abrecht, WCC, Geneva 1980.

13. *The Final Document on Justice, Peace and the Integrity of Creation*, Seoul, Republic of Korea, 5–12 March 1990, WCC, Geneva 1990.

3. *The Roman Catholic Church, Social Ethics and The Ecumenical Movement*

1. The 'Sword of the Spirit' movement in the UK in the 1939–45 war, which was strongly backed by Cardinal Hinsley, Archbishop of Westminster, came to grief partly because the Vatican in due course forbade Roman Catholics even to say the Lord's Prayer with other Christians. Today this seems incredible.

2. Cf. Paul Misnet, *Social Catholicism in Europe; from the Onset of Industrialization to the First World War*, Darton, Longman & Todd 1981.

3. Paragraph seventy-nine reads, 'It is indeed true, as history clearly proves, that owing to changed circumstances much that was formerly done by small groups can nowadays only be done by large associations. None the less, just as it is wrong to withdraw from the individual and

commit to a group what private enterprise and industry can accomplish, so too it is an injustice, and grave evil and a disturbance of right order, for a larger and higher association to arrogate to itself functions which can be performed effectively by smaller and lower societies. This is a fundamental principle of social philosophy unshakable and unchangeable.' Paragraph eighty calls this the principle of subsidiarity, and says if the State observes this it will be able to carry out with greater freedom its own tasks of direction, watching, stimulating and retraining. Clearly a wide range of activities is still called for by the State within these parameters.

4. Cf. P. McEntee, *The Social Catholic Movement in Great Britain*, Macmillan 1927.

5. *Instruction on Certain Aspects of Theology of Liberation* (1984), and *Instruction on Christian Freedom and Liberation* (1986).

6. If the WCC had done more in this area it would have had difficulty in reaching a consensus between most of the Orthodox and most of the rest of its constituency; that, of course, is no reason for not bringing them into dialogue.

7. On the social teaching of the Vatican, the *Dictionary of the Ecumenical Movement* is naturally not as useful as it is on the main area with which it is concerned, but one of its editors is a Roman Catholic, and it is useful as far as it goes. Further sources are *Proclaiming Justice and Peace: One Hundred Years of Catholic Social Teaching*, Collins, for CAFOD 1991; Jean-Yves Calvez, *The Church and Social Justice: The Social Teaching of the Popes from Leo XIII to Pius XI, 1878–1958*, ET Burns & Oates 1961; *The Gospel of Peace and Justice: Catholic Social Teaching since Pope John*, ed. J. Gremillion, Orbis, Maryknoll, New York 1975; Rodger Charles, *The Social Teaching of Vatican 2*, Plater Publications, Oxford 1982; D. Dorr, *Option for the Poor*, Gill & Macmillan 1983, revised edition 1988.

8. It was Leonardo Boff's book *Church, Charism and Power: Liberation Theology and the Institional Church*, ET SCM Press and Crossroad Publishing 1985 which chiefly got him into trouble with the Sacred Congregation for the Defence of the Faith and ended, first of all in his being silenced for a year, and subsequently in his decision to leave the priesthood.

9. Cf. Paul Tillich, *The Protestant Era*, Chicago University Press 1945.

10. Those who want to be introduced to it will find a vast literature. One well tried book is A.P. d'Entrèves, *Natural Law: An Introduction to Legal Philosophy*, Hutchinson, second edition 1970.

11. Cf R. A. McCormick, 'Moral Theology 1940–89: an Overview' in Theological Studies, (USA), vol.50, 1989.

12. Cf. T. S. Derr, *Barriers to Ecumenism: The Holy See and the World Council of Churches on Social Questions*, Orbis, Maryknoll, New York 1982.

13. Details of the SODEPAX documents referred to: *World Development; the Challenge to the Churches*, Beirut 1968; *The Challenge of Development; A sequel to the Beirut Conference*, Montreal 1969; *Towards a Theology of Development*, Cartigny, Geneva 1969; *Money in a Village World: The Interests of Developing Countries and International Monetary Reform*, Geneva 1970; *Partnership or Privilege: Ecumenical Reactions to the Second World Development Decade*, 1970. All these were published for SODEPAX from the Ecumenical Centre, Geneva. Other consultations included one on economic development in Asia (1970), and on peace in Northern Ireland (1973).

14. A lively account of the SODEPAX years 1968–71 is included in the autobiography of its first secretary, *King's Pawn: the Memoirs of George H. Dunne SJ*, Loyola University Press, Chicago 1990.

15. An instance of this is illuminating, even though it is not of major importance. It was originally intended to hold the consultation on 'Towards a Theology of Development' in Trinidad. It was in the Third World, and the Roman Catholic Archbishop of Trinidad was President of the Trinidad Council of Churches. The Vatican vetoed this and said it should be held in the Geneva area. The surmise is that the Vatican was nervous at what might emerge. In Trinidad it would have been an event of enormous local importance, local reporting of which might have been picked up by the world media beyond Trinidad. In the Geneva area, where so many international meetings take place, it would pass unnoticed.

4. *Critics from Without and Within*

1. The Cardiff Consultation on 'Violence, Non-Violence and the Struggle for Social Justice' (1971) is an example of the WCC listening to those rarely heard in person by the churches. Some actually engaged in guerrilla warfare against colonial overlords or militarily oppressive governments were present.

2. The Roman Catholic Church has had problems of a similar kind, for instance in what was Czeckoslovakia; it is not proving easy to reconcile those who took different attitudes during the communist period. China continues to exhibit differences in church attitudes to its government.

3. Cf. Karl Barth, *Against the Stream: Shorter Post-War Writings 1946–52*, ET SCM Press 1954, p.39.

4. David Martin, *A General Theory of Secularization,* Blackwell, Oxford 1978, pp.294f.

5. Cf. *Church and Society in the Late Twentieth Century: The Economic and Political Task,* SCM Press 1983, ch. 3; *The Future of Christian Ethics,* SCM Press 1987, ch. 5; *Religion and the Ambiguities of Capitalism,* SCM Press 1991, ch. 6, sections 1 and 2.

6. *Amsterdam to Nairobi: The World Council of Churches and the Third World,* Georgetown University Press, Washington DC, 1978.

7. *Who Speaks for the Churches? A Critique of the Geneva Conference on Church and Society,* St Andrew Press, Edinburgh and Abingdon Press, Nashville 1967.

8. Cf. *Two Kingdoms and One World,* ed. K. H. Hertz, Augsburg Press, Minneapolis 1976.

9. Cf. the claims of recent Papal Encyclicals that the church offers principles of reflection, criteria of judgment and directions for action (discussed in the previous chapter).

10. Cf. the discussion of a *status confessionis* below.

11. Cf. Richard Cobden who in the nineteenth century said, with reference to the repeal of the Corn Laws in the mid-forties, that it was the most important event in history since the coming of Christ.

12. *Global Economy: A Confessional Issue for the Churches,* WCC, Geneva 1983.

13. *Against the Stream,* ch. 4, (note 3 above).

14. *Costly Unity* 1993, issued jointly by the Unity and Renewal and the Justice, Peace and Integrity of Creation Units of the WCC.

15. Castro misunderstood the Open Letter as a call to moderation instead of 'taking sides'; he said moderation would involve the risk of neutrality or passiveness, bordering on indifference. On the contrary, he maintained, the WCC speaks out of dialogue and participation with those who suffer in their local situation. I discuss this again in Part Two.

16. The WCC did not comment on the Berlin document, but after the letter from Archbishop Habgood, following the Manchester meeting, the General Secretary suggested that five members of the group should meet him and four of his colleagues to explore the issues raised. This meeting took place at the Ecumenical Institute near Geneva in February 1994. Some account of it appeared in the April 1944 number of *One World,* the monthly journal of the WCC, written by the then editor. Useful as this was, it became clear that more clarification is needed if the procedures of the WCC study programme leading to the 1998 Assembly are to be modified, as compared with the years since Vancouver.

5. The Church and its Function in Society

1. Oldham, *The Church and its Function in Society*, pp.223 ff.

2. There were studies on non-theological factors affecting church unity by C.H. Dodd and others prior to the Faith and Order conference at Edinburgh in 1937, and by Walter Muelder and Nils Ehrenstrom prior to that at Montreal in 1963.

3. A famous study of the Southern Baptist Church in the USA showed that although it has a 'gathered church' ecclesiology, there is a powerful centralized bureaucracy, all the more so for being unavowed; see Paul Mansfield Harrison, *Authority and Power in the Free Church Tradition: A Social Case Study of the American Baptist Convention*, 1959, reprinted 1971, Carbunkle, Illinois. No such study has been made of the Curia. See also Mady Thun, *The Precarious Organization: Sociological Explanations of the Churches' Mission and Structure*, Monton, The Hague 1976.

4. The treatment in recent years of such Roman Catholic theologians as Edward Schillebeeckx, Charles Curran and Leonardo Boff by the Sacred Congregation for Defence of the Faith has raised this question.

5. Cf. Charles Granfield, *Ecclesial Cybernetics: a Study of Democracy in the Church*, Macmillan 1973; Peter Rudge, *Ministry and Management: The Study of Ecclesiastical Administration*, Tavistock 1968; Peter de Haas, *The Church as Institution: Critical Studies in the Relation between Theology and Sociology*, Jornker, Apeldoorn 1972; 'The Church as Institution' ed. G. Baum and A. Greeley, *Concilium* 1974.

6. *Ecumenism in Transition: A Paradigm Shift in the Ecumenical Movement*, WCC, Geneva 1991.

7. Julio de Santa Ana, Ulrich Duckrow and Konrad Raiser, *The Political Economy of the Holy Spirit*, WCC Geneva 1991. It will be discussed in chapter 7.

8. The loss of confidence, for whatever reasons, is serious as far as the young are concerned. The WCC youth work has steadily declined over the past thirty years. From where are the imaginative and creative Christian youth and students to come as delegates to the 1998 Assembly, and who will they represent? This issue of course goes back from the WCC to the churches themselves.

Part Two: Present and Future

6. Where We are Today 1: Three Issues

1. Nationalism is mainly a phenomenon of the last 200 years, though it often gives itself the air of great antiquity. Today almost every-

one regards their national identity as being as much part of their self-identification as their sex. The idea that each nation should have the right to be a sovereign state is equally modern. What constitutes a nation is a mystery. There are no clear criteria. Language is often considered to be one, but Switzerland has four. We are reduced to saying that if a group of people feel they belong together and consitute a nation, then they are one. (cf. Benedict Anderson, *Imagined Communities*, Verso 1983). But it does not follow that they must constitute a separate state. Nationalism in Europe has produced two world wars this century. One can see that it can be a constructive force as against tribalism, but it seems too narrow an entity, whilst a world state is a dream (or perhaps a nightmare). Humankind is fumbling for something in between. The Marxist notion that nationalism is one of the manipulative tools of the possessing classes to maintain their power is too simple, yet governments do continually find that whipping up nationalist fervour diverts criticism from them. Nationalism needs relativizing. One would expect Christian theology to relativize it, and yet the Christian church has frequently found, and still finds, that the easiest way to popularity is to embody and sanctify nationalism. As far as the Bible is concerned, cultural diversity is approved on the whole, and the state is given strong endorsement on the whole, but the nation has no political status in it. Recent work of the WCC takes nation-states for granted, and does not help in elucidating these issues. (On this general theme cf. Ernest Gellner, *Nations and Nationalism*, Blackwell 1983, and Eric Hobsbawn, *Nations and Nationalism Since 1788*, CUP 1990).

On war, revolution and counter-revolution one cannot blame the WCC for not resolving the differences between the minority of pacifists among Christians and the majority who are not. But it tends not to bring out the issues clearly by producing statements which are supposed to be agreed, but tend in a pacifist direction because they do not differentiate between force and violence; nor do they illuminate the principles of discrimination (on deontological ethical reasoning) and proportion (based on consequentialist reasoning) in the Just War doctrine, nor bring it to bear on the military issues in international relations (including those of the UN), and guerrilla civil warfare. Advocating non-violent cultures, if the details can be spelled out, is a challenging goal, but it still does not exclude the question of force. Non-violence is sometimes used with such a wide reference as to include everything that hinders human fulfilment. Greater clarity and precision is called for. On racism, to which the WCC has given a lot of attention, it cannot be faulted for stressing white racism, for whites mostly have the power. But it would bring out the insidious nature of racism, as well as being more challenging to some of its constituents, if more attention were given to yellow, brown and black racism.

2. On this issue see my *Religion and the Ambiguities of Capitalism*, SCM Press 1991 chs 3–6.

3. Changes in the British National Health Service have reduced the power of consultants.

4. In various books of which a trilogy *Law, Legislation and Liberty*, Routledge and Kegan Paul 1973–79.

5. Most discussions in recent years on justice as fairness have arisen from John Rawl's *A Theory of Justice*, OUP 1972.

6. 'The Political Economy of the Holy Spirit', WCC Geneva 1990.

7. 'Christian Faith and the World Economy Today', WCC Geneva 1992.

8. *North-South, A Programme for Survival*, 1980, and *Common Crisis, North-South: Co-operation for World Recovery*, 1983.

9. *Our Common Future*, the Report of the World Commission on Environment and Development, OUP 1987.

10. *Environmentally Sustainable Economic Development: Building on Brundtland*, ed. Robert Goodland, Herman Daly, Salah el Serafy and Bernd von Droste. Three of the authors had previously written a report for the World Bank, 'Ten Reasons why Northern Income Growth is not the Solution for Southern Poverty'. To put 'Building on Brundtland' in the title of this later booklet is deliberately ingenuous, for they are contradicting it. The World Energy Council has produced a report *Energy for To-Morrow's World*, St Martin's Press 1993, which argues that the world population is now 5.5 million and by 2120 it will be 8 million, 85% of them in poor countries; without more energy resources they will lack basic necessities, so energy should not be subsidized, which encourages wastefulness, nor the search for new sources be frustrated.

11. 'The State of the World's Children', OUP 1992. Malnutrition, like infected water, aggravates diseases like measles, diarrhoea and pneumonia. The cost of an antibiotic against pneumonia is just twenty pence.

12. Tim Lang and Colin Hines, *The New Protectionism*, Earthscan 1992.

13. Social policy issues will no doubt be tackled differently in the different types of market economies. In the USA shareholders are more influential, in Japan, managers, and western Europe has social market institutions. The European Union has seen a hugh rise in productivity but also a steady rise in unemployment. National incomes have risen by 90% between 1970 and 1990 but jobs by only 7%. Changes are needed in the labour market, partly by better retraining schemes, partly by developing a

better infrastructure in the various countries of the European Union, and partly by an increase in personal service jobs which is badly needed, but for which electorates must be willing to pay. In any case governments must spend more, or see that more is spent, on environmental issues. Years at work will also be fewer, and cover the years 20 to 55 (or 60 at the most).

14. There is no reason in principle to object to the advocacy of vested interests. Persons and groups are the best judges of their own interests as they understand them, and are entitled to present them in the public forum. But they must be prepared for scrutiny, and to allow for the fact that others also have interests to which they must be prepared to listen, so that some tolerable adjustment in policy can be made between them for the present. This is what is meant by the 'common good'.

15. Cf. *Letters and Papers from Prison*, third revised and enlarged edition, SCM Press 1967.

16. The Human Fertilization and Embryology Authority in the UK is seeking public opinion on whether eggs from aborted foetuses or corpses should be used in fertility treatment.

17. The Club of Rome is a private body, mainly of natural scientists, whose first report in 1972, *The Limits to Growth*, created something of a sensation. It predicted that the world's resources of tin, mercury, zinc, copper and lead would be exhausted by 1993. It assumed exponential growth in consumption but not in technology.

18. The WCC quickly published a useful summary and comment, *Redeeming the Creation: The Rio Earth Summit: Challenges for the Churches*, Wesley Granberg-Michaelson 1992.

19. It is odd that Moltmann aligns God the Spirit with Gaia in his *God in Creation*, SCM Press and Harper 1985 (pp. 17–19, 300).

20. One of the most rigorous advocates of animal rights, among many, is Tom Regan, *The Case for Animal Rights*, Berkeley and Los Angeles University Press 1983; in the UK, Andrew Linzey is the most persistent writer on animal rights, e.g. *Christianity and the Rights of Animals*, SPCK 1987, *Animal Theology*, SCM Press 1994 and other books.

21. Cf. *The Community of Women and Men in the Church: The Sheffield Report*, ed. Constance F. Parvey, WCC 1983, p. 145. Many others have taken up this point, in an extended form, e.g. Rosemary Radford Ruether, *Gaia and God*, SCM Press and Harper 1993.

22. Of the many books on feminist theology perhaps Elizabeth Schüssler Fiorenza, *In Memory of Her*, SCM Press and Crossroad Publishing 1983, may be singled out.

7. *Where We are Today* 2: *The Recent Slogan and its Predecessors*

1 Reinhold Niebuhr, *The Children of Light and the Children of Darkness*, Nisbet 1945, p. vi.

2. On these consultations, and the slogans, see the *Dictionary of the Ecumenical Movement* (above Introduction, n.2).

3. In ch. 2 of a symposium *Technology and Social Justice*, edited by me, SCM Press 1971.

4. 'Perspectives on Political Ethics'. On this and on connected matters like Minjung Theology, see the *Dictionary* (note 2 above).

5. Cf. *Selection from the Prison Notebooks*, ed. G. Hoare and G. Nowell-Smith, Lawrence and Wishart 1971.

6. An independent enquiry was sponsored in the UK by Christian Aid, and it bears out this comment, *Responding to Poverty: Perspectives from the Church*, 1994.

7. 'The Historical Roots of our Ecological Crisis', in Science USA, March 1967.

8. Keith Thomas, *Man and the Natural World: Changing Attitudes in England 1500–1800*, Allen Lane 1983. There are exceptions, e.g. Thomas Traherne.

9. *homoousios* which in English becomes 'of one substance' in the 'Nicene' Creed, referring to the relation of Father and Son in the Godhead.

10. I have been quoting here from a WCC Press Release in reply to an attack by *The Reader's Digest* on the worship conducted by Professor Chung of Korea at the Canberra Assembly, as syncretistic; the journal was taking up criticisms made at the time. Talk of 'thinking like a mountain' probably derives from the work of the 'deep ecologist' Norwegian Philosopher, Arne Naess.

11. Cf. Robert Murray SJ, *The Cosmic Covenant*, Sheed & Ward 1992.

12. Cf. John Macmurray, *The Form of the Personal*, Vol. 1: *The Self as Agent*, Faber 1957; Vol. 2: *Persons in Relation*, Faber 1961: and Jacques Maritain, *True Humanism*, ET Bles 1938, and *The Person and the Common Good*, Bles 1947.

13. Cf. John Mahoney, *The Making of Moral Theology: a Study of the Roman Catholic Tradition*, Clarendon Press, Oxford 1987.

14. *Redeeming the Creation*, Wesley Granberg-Michaelson, WCC 1992.

15. The ecumemical memory is short; the post-Uppsala attempt to co-ordinate WCC work, the Humanum Study, has gone into oblivion.

16. There has been little effort to give doctrinal clarity to the term

Integrity; the best example is a paper by Professor Douglas John Hall of Montreal, 'Biblical and Theological Background of the Term' in a Church and Society document Reintegrating God's Creation, WCC, 1987. My own tentative suggestion is that creation, with its ambiguities, is as God intended if human life as we experience it, (with its own ambiguities), were to be possible. It is the ambiguities which raise doubts and make a theodicy necessary.

8. *Where We are Today 3: Contending Theologies*

1. Of Niebuhr's books the ones to mention are the early *Moral Man and Immoral Society*, 1932; first English edition SCM Press 1963, and his Gifford Lectures *The Nature and Destiny of Man*, Vol. 1: *Human Nature*, 1941, Vol.2: *Human Destiny*, Nisbet 1943.

2. Quoted in Christopher Hill, *The English Bible and the Seventeenth Century Revolution*, Allen Lane, Penguin Press 1993.

3. John Murray, *Principles of Conduct*, Tyndale Press, 1957; that author was Professor of Systematic Theology at Westminster Theological Seminary, Philadelphia.

4. Cf. my article 'The Kingdom of God: Political and Social Theology' in *The Blackwell Encyclopaedia of Modern Christian Thought*, ed. Alistair McGrath, Oxford 1993.

5. Quoted from an article in *Grypho*, 1977, in Christopher Norris, *The Contest of Faculties: Philosophy and Theory after Deconstruction*, Methuen 1985; cf. the same author's *Deconstruction: Theory and Practice*, rev. ed. Routledge 1991.

6. On Dependency Theory I am much indebted to an article 'Liberating Liberation Theology: Towards Independence from Dependency Theory' by Peter G. Moll in *Journal of Theology for South Africa*, March 1992. Nearly all Latin American Liberation Theologians assume the theory; so does Franz J. Hinkelammert in *The Ideoligical Weapons of Death; A Theological Critique of Capitalism*, Orbis, Mary Knoll, New York 1986, from a more social science approach.

7. I say nothing about multi-national corporations in this book, not because I hold any special brief for them and, indeed, I consider it to be a serious issue how they can be made accountable in some international framework, and whether big institutional investors in them can be more active. But their importance in the whole picture is often exaggerated, and they become too easy a target, concentrating on which fails to come to grips with important issues of trade and domestic policies in both the First and Third Worlds.

8. 'Instruction on Certain Aspects of the Theology of Liberation' 1984, and 'Instruction on Christian Freedom and Liberation', 1986.

9. Published in the UK by the Catholic Institute for International Relations.

10. A most implausible assertion by Moltmann; one has only to consider Judaism.

11. Cf. 'The Christian Gospel and Social Responsibility: the Eastern Orthodox Tradition in History', John Meyendorff, in *Continuity and Discontinuity in Church History*, ed. F. F. Church and Timothy George, Brill, Leiden 1971.

12. Cf. Stanley S. Harakas, *Contemporary Moral Issues Facing the Orthodox Christian*, Light and Life Publishing Company, Minneapolis, Minnesota 1982.

13. *De Trinitate*, 5.10.

14. Cf. Leonard Hodgson, *The Doctrine of the Trinity*, Nisbet 1944; Jürgen Moltmann, The Trinity and the Kingdom: the Doctrine of God, SCM Press and Westminster Press 1981, where he writes of three consciousnesses and three wills, and *opposes* the Trinity to monotheism; in *God in Creation*, SCM Press and Harper 1985, he says each subject of the Trinity possesses a unique personality; cf. Leonardo Boff, *Trinity and Society*, Orbis, MaryKnoll, New York 1981, where God becomes a co-operative society. Feminists are attracted to it and are attacking more 'monarchical' and less 'social' conceptions of the Trinity as patriarchal, which is to misunderstand Trinitanian doctrine.

15. It was a product of a small working party, written up by Ulrich Duckrow, Konrad Raiser and Julio de Santa Ana, Geneva 1990.

16. One element in the attack on instrumental reason may be the work of Max Horkeimer of the Frankfurt School of Culturally Orientated Marxism. He refers to 'instrumental rationality', the never-ceasing pursuit of the most technically effective means for advancing goals that are not themselves examined because they are felt to be agreed upon, the results of subjective choices, unchangeable, or for some reason 'given'. Cf. *Critique of Instrumental Reason*, ET 1974, Seabury, New York. Habermas himself is not willing to grant to religion any public truth claims.

17. On the debate cf. Bernard Hoose, *Proportionalism*, Georgetown University Press, Washington DC 1987; Richard McCormick, *Doing Evil to Achieve Good*, Loyola University Press, Chicago 1978; Vincent MacNamara, *Faith and Ethics*, Gill & Macmillan, Dublin 1978. Among traditionalists cf. German Grisez, *The Way of the Lord Jesus*, Franciscan Herald Press, Chicago 1987; John Finnis, *Fundamental of Ethics*, OUP, 1983. Among revisionists cf. Bernard Häring, *Free and Faithful in Christ*,

3 vols, ET St Paul's Press 1978, 1979 and 1981, and any of the books of Charles Curran, e.g. *Transition and Tradition in Moral Theology*, University of Notre Dame Press, Indiana 1974.

9. *Questions of Methods in Christian Social Ethics*

1. I have dealt more fully with prophecy in chapter 5, 'Problems of Prophecy' in *Church and Society in the Late Twentieth Century*, SCM Press 1983, when after discussing its role in the Bible and the church I turn to prophecy and the life of faith.

2. The conferences of the Division on World Mission and Evangelism of the WCC at Bangkok, Melbourne and San Antonio show many signs of this, so that there is as much confusion in this area as in social ethics. On those conferences see the *Dictionary of the Ecumenical Movement* (above introduction, n. 2).

3. H. Richard Niebuhr, *Christ and Culture*, Faber 1952. The five types are (1) Christ against Culture (e.g. Tertullian, Tolstoy; (2) The Christ of Culture (e.g. Abelard, Ritschl; (3) Christ above Culture (e.g. Clement of Alexandria, St Thomas Aquinas); (4) Christ and Culture in Paradox (e.g. Luther, Kierkegaard); (5) Christ the Transformer of Culture (e.g. Calvin, F.D. Maurice). I do not think this typology has been bettered.

4. *Octogesima Adveniens*, Apostolic Letter of His Holiness Pope Paul VI to Maurice, Cardinal Roy, President of the Council of the Laity and of the Pontifical Commission for Justice and Peace on the occasion of the Eightieth Anniversary of the Encyclical *Rerum Novarum*, par. 4.

5. Quoted in Paul Ramsey, *The Just War*, Scribner 1968, p.391 and two other places, but without detailed reference. cf. Aquinas, *Summa Theologiae*, 1a, 2ae qu. 4.4.

6. The only place where the subject is systematically presented is Appendix 2 'Middle Axioms in Christian Social Ethics' in the book referred to in note 1 above.

7. W. A. Visser't Hooft and J. H. Oldman, *The Church and its Function in Society*, Allen & Unwin, 1937, p.219.

8. *Perspectives on Political Ethics*, WCC Geneva, 1987. Krisang was closely involved in the Cyprus Consultation referred to in chapter 7.

9. Ideology in the Marxist sense dates from Marx's *The German Ideology*, 1846. A classic book refining the concept was Karl Mannheim, *Ideology and Utopia*, Routledge 1936; and using it in a Christian context, Reinhold Niebuhr, *Moral Man and Immoral Society*, SCM Press 1962, ch. 6 (Scribner, New York 1932). There has been an immense discussion of the whole issue in the sociology of knowledge ever since. John Milbank

in *Theology and Social Theory: Beyond Secular Reason*, Blackwell 1990, comes close to saying that there are no sociological facts independent of a total ideology.

   10. Cf. 'Violence, Non-violence and the Struggle for Social Justice', Report of the Cardiff Consultation, 1971, *Ecumenical Review*, vol. 25, no. 4, 1973. Also the report of a follow-up consultation in Corymeela, N. Ireland on 'Violence, Non-violence and Civil Conflict', WCC 1983.

   11. Cf. 'Risk Decision and Moral Values', John Elford in *The Nuclear Weapons Debate: Theological and Ethical Issues*, ed. Richard Bauckham and John Elford, SCM Press 1989, ch. 10.

   12. 'Faith, Science and the Future' Conference at MIT, Vol.2 of the report *Faith and Science in an Unjust Society*, ed. Paul Abrecht, WCC Geneva 1980, Section 10 Report 'Towards a New Christian Social Ethic and New Social Policies for the Church'.

   13. Cf. the tone of two recent reports on climate issues: *Accelerated Climate Change: Sign of Peril, Test of Faith*, WCC Geneva 1944, and *Energy*, a report of the Churches Energy Group in the UK (*Christian Action Journal*, London, January 1994); the former is much more extreme.

10. *Looking to the Future in Ecumenical Social Ethics*

   1. Jan Kerkofs SJ, 'Will the Churches meet the Europeans?', *The Tablet*, 18 September 1993.

   2. Cf. Brunner's main ethical work, *The Divine Imperative*, ET Lutterworth Press 1937, (German title, *Das Gebot und die Ordnungen*); Barth's main ethical work is *Church Dogmatics*, Vol.3, Part 4, ET T. & T. Clark 1961. Both were Reformed, not Lutheran, theologians.

   3. The work of Stanley Hauerwas is very influential in this area; two of his books are *Vision and Virtue: Essays in Christian Ethical Reflection*, Fides Publishers, Notre Dame, Indiana 1974, and *The Peaceable Kingdom: A Primer of Christian Ethics*, University of Notre Dame and SCM Press 1984.

   4. Cf. the essay 'The State of the Ark: Lessons from Seoul' by Douglas John Hall in *Between the Ark and the Rainbow*, ed. D.Priman Niles, WCC 1992.

   5. For most of this paragraph I am indebted to 'The Metaphysics of Environmental Concern: a Critique of Ecotheological Antidualism', Bronislaw Szerkzynski, *Studies in Christian Ethics*, Vol. 6 no. 2, 1933. It states concisely considerations which I have had in mind for some time, and clarified my mind.

   6. The informal group met in Vancouver in 1990, Berlin in 1992 and

Manchester in 1993. After the Berlin meeting a pamphlet was published privately for general circulation, 'The Future of Ecumenical Social Thought'; after the Manchester meeting a reasoned letter was sent by Dr John Habgood, Archbishop of York (who chaired it) to Dr Konrad Raiser, the new General Secretary of the WCC. It has not been made public, but it is not confidential, and a few people have seen it.

7. The Report of the Seventh Assembly of the World Council of Churches, Canberra 1993, ed. Michael Kinnamon, WCC Geneva 1993.

8. *Ecumenism in Transition: A Paradigm Shift in the Ecumenical Movement*, WCC Geneva 1991.

9. *Costly Unity*, WCC Geneva 1993. Periodic joint activities between Faith and Order and 'Life and Work' sides of the WCC are clearly to be welcomed, but the presence of Faith and Order representatives does not serve as a correction of one-sided and simplistic work on the 'Life and Work' side. They are admirable in their own field, but they have not the experience in social ethics and the Christian witness in society. *Costly Unity* shows that they were unable to deal with the deficiences of Seoul and the exaggerated claims for it. Better procedures can come only from within the 'Life and Work' side itself.

10. In this book I have made a theological assumption that human beings in the common experience of living touch a reality beyond themselves; that they ask the same basic questions about their lives, and that these are the significant questions to ask. Further, that the Christian faith gives a more adequate interpretation of what is in many ways mysterious, than any other interpretation, but that its verification can only be sought in human experience. There are theological trends today which deny this. Influenced by the later philosophical work of Wittgenstein on 'language games', narrative theologians regard the Christian narrative as highly specific to particular communities, so that doubt is cast on common values as against a distinctively Christian understanding, in social theology and ethics. As far as I know the WCC has not explicitly dealt with these differences, but they probably underlie the ambiguities in *Costly Unity*.

A Note on Further Reading

Documentation on the work of the WCC is extensive, especially when regional events are included; that of the Roman Catholic Church in this area rather less so, because it is so centralized. As far as the WCC is concerned, apart from the proceedings of Assemblies, and the minutes of Committees, it published in 1983 a list *Six Hundred Ecumenical Consultations 1948–82*, by Ans van der Bent, who was then Librarian at the Ecumenical Centre, Geneva. Those few who are able to engage in detailed work on the Ecumenical Movement are likely to find this library indispensable. The rest, who wish to read further on it, will find the *Dictionary of the Ecumenical Movement*, with its articles and bibliographies, their best source. I refer to it in the Preface and give details in note 2 of the Introductory chapter. I had intended to include here a Select Bibliography of books for further reading. Over the years I have accumulated a large bibliography, and to print all of it would be daunting and unnecessary. However, I have found it impossible to find a basis for selecting some two dozen books for special notice. To cover the different facets of the issues raised could not be done within that compass, and would be arbitrary. The notes to the chapters indicate the sources I have found most immediately useful, and they form a kind of Select Bibliography.

Writings 1991–94

1991
'Christian Ethics', *A Companion to Ethics* ed. Peter Singer, Blackwell, Oxford.

'Catholic Social Thought: *Rerum Novarum* after 100 Years', *One World*, World Council of Churches, No. 168, August/September.

1992
'Centesimus Annus: an Appraisal', *Theology*, November.

'A Christian Slant on Basic Income', *Basic Income Research Bulletin*, July.

'Remembering Reinhold Niebuhr (1892–1971)', Theology Themes, vol. 1, No. 2, Northern Baptist College, Manchester8.

1993
'Business Ethics and the Pastoral Task', *The Way*, July.

'Christian Socialism'; and 'The Kingdom of God in Contemporary Political and Social Theology', *Encyclopedia of Modern Christian Thought*, ed. Alister McGrath, Blackwell, Oxford.

'The Four Principles and Their Use: the Possibilities of Agreement between different Faiths and Ideologies', *Principles of Health Care Ethics*, ed. Raanan Gillon, John Wiley, Chichester.

1994
'The Protestant Work Ethic: What was it? Is its ghost still around?' *Business Ethics*, Vol. 3, No. 1, January.

'Christian Capitalism or Christian Socialism? The Moral Order of a Free Society', with Michael Novak, Institute of Economic Affairs.

'*Veritatis Splendor*: a Comment', *Studies in Christian Ethics*, Vol. 7, no. 2.

'William Temple: the Man and his Impact on Church and Society', Gresham College, London, and the William Temple Foundation, Manchester.

Index